I0037561

The

MONARCH

The Signature 8 Method for Launching Your Dream Business with Clarity, Confidence & Love

Copyright @ 2022 Amanda Wilson-Ciocci

The Monarch: The Signature 8 Method for Launching Your Dream Business with Clarity, Confidence & Love

YGTMedia Co. Trade Paperback Edition.

ISBN trade paperback: 978-1-989716-77-9

eBook: 978-1-989716-79-3

All Rights Reserved. No part of this book can be scanned, distributed, or copied without permission. This book or any portion thereof may not be reproduced or used in any manner whatsoever without the express written permission of the publisher at publishing@ygtmedia.co—except for the use of brief quotations in a book review.

The author has made every effort to ensure the accuracy of the information within this book was correct at time of publication. The author does not assume and hereby disclaims any liability to any party for any loss, damage, or disruption caused by errors or omissions, whether such errors or omissions result from accident, negligence, or any other cause. This book is not intended to be a substitute for the medical advice of a licensed physician. The reader should consult with their doctor in any matters relating to their health.

The publisher is not responsible for websites (or their content) that are not owned by the publisher.

Published in Canada, for Global Distribution by YGTMedia Co. www.ygtmedia.co/publishing

To order additional copies of this book: publishing@ygtmedia.co

Interior design and typesetting by Doris Chung

Cover design by Michelle Fairbanks

eBook by Ellie Sipilä

Author Photo by Helen Tansey Photography

TORONTO

Dedicated to Kiel, Koen, Giulia, and Luca
I love you to the moon and back . . .
Always and forever.
xoxoxo

To the mentors in my life who were anchors in times of fear and storm,
who illuminated the way and gifted me with a spark and the possibility of
transformation.
And to my mom, who picked up the phone and ignited a spark.
Thank you!

The
MONARCH

The Signature 8 Method for
Launching Your Dream Business
with Clarity, Confidence & Love

AMANDA WILSON-CIOCCI

Table of Contents

To my readers:
This is not just a business book.
This is you giving yourself the space to know yourself better, listen to and own your inner voice, and learn how to share your gifts with the world.
You are here for a reason.
Own your amazingness, do it differently, and do it your way.
You've got this.

THE MONARCH

YOU ARE ALWAYS ONE DECISION AWAY FROM A TOTALLY DIFFERENT LIFE.

Happiness is as a butterfly, which, when pursued, is always just beyond your grasp, but which, if you will sit down quietly, may alight upon you.

Nathaniel Hawthorne

I have always loved this saying, which was stitched onto fabric in my grandmother's home. She filled her space with monarch references, even keeping a preserved monarch in a glass dish in her china cabinet. I never knew exactly what it meant, but assumed it was a Scottish superstition. I was close with my grandma—I loved our tea-filled afternoons, her Scottish accent, and the way she and my granda would break into dance together when a song by Louis Armstrong or Frank Sinatra was playing.

When I was twenty-one years old, I lost my grandma to cancer. One year later, I was diagnosed with thyroid cancer myself. To say I was scared was an understatement. I remember sitting in the London hospital waiting for radiation treatment, flipping through a pamphlet that read, "What is Thyroid Cancer?" Numbly, I turned to the back page and noticed the symbol for thyroid cancer is a butterfly. Although I had not yet had my treatment and didn't know what the outcome would be, I knew at that moment everything was going to be okay.

When I started this business, I struggled to come up with a name, something I'll dive into in the Know It chapter. In desperation, I asked my husband, Kiel, to help me pick a name. He pointed outside the window and said, "Look . . . a *monarch*," and I immediately knew and felt the significance.

Here at The Monarch and Co., the monarch represents transformation and how we help entrepreneurs. They are welcomed into the cocoon: a safe space where they can break down (if necessary), build, and grow, so that when they are ready, they can spread their wings and do what they are meant to do in this world.

As the wise Maya Angelou once said, "We delight in the beauty of the butterfly, but rarely admit the changes it has gone through to achieve that beauty." At The Monarch & Co., we acknowledge and celebrate those changes.

This life is meant to be lived and you have a purpose in it. You have a gift to share with the world and sharing it has purpose. My goal is to illuminate your path, guide you along the journey, and help you reach your highest potential so that when you launch your heart baby out into the world, it will make a bigger and better impact. It's the butterfly effect and why the monarch is significant.

My driving passion is to empower and inspire you, guide you along your path, and leave you with the possibility of transformation so you can get your work out there. The world needs your vibrant voice, creations, color, and innovation. And for my role in that . . . I am both excited and honored to do this work and hold the space for your transformation.

A NOTE TO THE READER

As you journey through this book, keep this idea from the Bhagavad Gita in mind: It is better to follow your own path, however imperfectly, than to follow someone else's perfectly.

There will be moments in this book when the words and the guidance will resonate so deeply with you, but there may be other moments when they don't and you feel they don't fit with how you would want or need to transform. My advice: take what you take and leave the rest.

The magic in the journey happens when you discover what possibilities lie within you and you gain the clarity and confidence to share it with the world. Because the world needs you.

This book will give you a road map to launch your work out into the world. I'll share my journey and what I know works, but this is less about my journey and more about yours.

There is no *one* business- or life-inspiring book that has guided my journey. There are many. Each book I've consumed has gifted me with gold nuggets I carry on to the next chapter, and they've inspired me to continue learning and growing. Let this book do that for you. Search for the gold nuggets, play in the "what if," and know that everything you need is already within you. Sometimes you just need a little spark to illuminate it!

BUT AMANDA, I HATE LAUNCHING

You don't hate launching. You just hate how you've been launching or the thought of launching in a way that doesn't feel aligned with you.

Maybe it's that you haven't found a way to launch that has worked for you and your business. Maybe you haven't found a system that gives you the step-by-step guidance to walk you through a launch that actually works. Or maybe you don't have the tools and resources to take care of the nitty-gritty aspects of your launch so that you can focus on your unique ability, the big picture, and serving your audience!

It's the reason I created the Signature 8 Method. It's a method I've crafted over the years to help entrepreneurs grow, scale, and launch online in a way that is aligned with their needs.

It's the method I use for myself, my clients, and my students, and the method I've seen create amazing results!

SIGNATURE 8 METHOD

Dream It: Dream of the life you want to live.

Know It: Understand why you are doing what you are doing.

Be It: Dig deep into your core values and align your business with your life.

Give It: Understand who you serve and who is most ideal for you.

Build It: Lay a strong foundation so you can scale with ease and speed.

Reach It: Connect and effectively reach your ideal audience.

Launch It: Launch your work out into the world with clarity and confidence.

Love It: Have gratitude for the journey and implement practices that are sustainable and spark joy!

A NOTE ABOUT CLIENTS VS. STUDENTS

In this book, I talk about both my students and clients, as there is a distinction between them.

Monarch students are entrepreneurs who have joined Monarch Business Academy (MBA), my three-month-long business, mindset, and launch accelerator signature program. There, we work through the Signature 8 Method to build and launch a business and life you love. While each chapter of this book works through each of these steps, the program dives deeper and provides so much more. If you're interested in the program, you can learn more at:

https://www.monarchbusinessacademy.com/MBA

Monarch clients are 1:1 coaching clients, Deep Dive & Roadmap session clients, and clients of our full-service digital marketing agency.

If you want to get organized, focused, and have a step-by-step road map to build your business and launch with clarity and confidence, stick with me!

Each day you are given a blank canvas. As artist Paul Gardner said, "A painting is never finished— it simply stops in interesting places." Let's get painting!

DREAM IT

Sometimes on the way to your dream, you get lost and find a better one.

Lisa Hammond

Did you ever lie in the grass as a kid, looking up at the sky to find shapes in the clouds? This is one of my favorite memories from when I was little. I remember all the sensual elements of the experience . . . lying in the grass with the warm sun shining down, smelling the warm earth beneath me, hearing the birds sing around me, looking up at the big blue sky. All the while making shapes out of the puffy, white clouds.

I would watch the shapes dance by, and time seemed to slow down. I would lose myself in that space, playing with my big visions. If I close my eyes and remember those moments, it's almost as if I'm there again.

Do you remember when you last allowed yourself to play with your big visions? To get lost in time and dream about the world around you? To dream about how you want to feel, what you want to see, and how to create that out of thin air?

It's a space I get to play in every day and it's the space I want to show you; one where dreams are dusted off and you get to live and play in possibility, making shapes out of clouds and turning dreams into reality. Ready?

DIVING IN

One of the first places I start when I work with entrepreneurs is what I like to call their Deep Dive & Roadmap session. This is a 1:1 deep dive where we go over all parts of your business; from the big vision to the nitty-gritty, we cover it all. It's a transformative session that changes you from feeling stuck and overwhelmed to having clarity and focus.

> GOLD *nugget* — Clarity and focus are your scarcest resources as an entrepreneur.

Meet Debi. Before our deep dive, she was "all over the map," going in circles over what to do next with her business. After only two hours of thorough, insightful, and thought-provoking questions, Debi felt calm and confident. She now had a clear road map and a new sense of direction and purpose for her life and her business. She understood how everything is interconnected, and she left saying, "This is simply the best investment I have made for me and my business."

Sometimes all you need is a few hours, an ounce of clarity, and a road map.

One of the first and most important questions I ask in this session is: What does success look like for you? We all have our own versions of success. Some want the big house and white picket fence with fancy cars, while others want to sit on a beach, own nothing, and have all the time in the world. The key is to know what *your* success looks like. Where do you want to be in three years' time in your life and business? In ten years, how are you spending your time and who are you spending it with? The clearer we are about what your success looks like, the easier it will be to put a plan together to achieve it.

This is often a challenging question for many. The first answers I get usually allude to the obvious—the freedom of time and money; the ability to vacation and do fun things with those you love when you want to; maybe indulging in more self-care.

These are surface-level answers. Still real and important, and definitely part of the vision of success, but the point of this session is to dive deep. And in order to do that, you need to be able to dream big.

DREAM BIG

Building your dream business and life is a big deal. It takes time, dedication, and a whole lot of passion to stay the course and see it through. If you don't have strong foundations in place or understand why you are doing what you are doing and what motivates you, then it's going to be a long, scenic road ahead. And while I love the scenic route when traveling, in business, I am all about taking the optimized route!

Many entrepreneurs skip this step of dreaming big, operating with surface-level visions. They see a general idea of success and want the result. But without strong foundations in place, you won't get far . . . and you may even find yourself looping back to where you first began.

> **GOLD** *nugget* Don't skip ahead. The nitty-gritty work may at times feel trivial, yet it is so foundational to the big picture and your long-term success.

I invite you to make a commitment while reading this, to give yourself permission to dive deep! Let's lie in the grass, play with your big visions, and get lost in time. It's time to dust off those dreams and make them a reality!

One of my favorite questions to follow up with after asking about what success looks like is: If you snapped your fingers (think along the lines of Mary Poppins here) and started living your dream life right now, what would it look like?

How are you spending your time? Who are you spending it with? How do you wake up in the mornings? What time do you wake up? Where are you? What do you smell? What do you see? How do you feel? What does your day look like? How much (or how little) are you working? What kinds of food do you eat? What do you look forward to most in your day?

> GOLD *nugget* — The more real our dreams feel, the more real they will become.

VISION BOARDS

Vision boards are my jam! Maybe it's the artist in me. I love seeing something abstract become reality. Vision boards are the beginning of crafting your reality and you get to be the artist of your own life. You can't expect to create a masterpiece by staring at the canvas or create your dream life by handing the brush over to someone else. You need to create it!

As my fabulous publishing team and writing coach would say when I was writing this book, "We can't edit blank pages, Amanda."

> **GOLD** *nugget* — You need to do the work and the work starts with your vision.

Remember making collages as a kid? Remember looking through old magazines, cutting out pictures that sparked joy or made you think of somewhere dreamy? Maybe a gorgeous island getaway or your dream house? Maybe I was the only forty-year-old living in a nine-year-old's body, but I loved making collages of what my future would look like. I only wish I had saved one to look at now! Thankfully with modern technology, you can save your vision boards, reduce waste, and avoid sticky fingers—thank you, Pinterest!

Visual representations of your dreams and goals, whether pasted on bristol board or pinned to a Pinterest board, are a great tool when creating your dream vision.

Why?

Because your vision and the clarity with which you see it matters. It's possible to transform your dreams into reality. All you need is the belief that your vision is possible and a plan to make that vision a reality.

Oprah, one of the most influential women in the world, says this about big visions: "Create the highest, grandest vision possible for your life, because you become what you believe."

So, let's do it! Let's create the highest, grandest vision possible for your life. Whether you use Pinterest or good old-fashioned scissors and glue, get it out of your brain!

If writing is your thing instead, write it out in a journal in *serious detail*! We are going after the nitty-gritty here. When you cut and paste your images or write out your big vision, it needs serious detail. Record what you are wearing, who you are with, what you are eating, what you are seeing and smelling. I want this vision to *feel* real. The more real it feels, the more real it will become.

Did you know that at the beginning of his career, Canadian actor Jim Carrey wrote himself a check for $10 million for "acting services rendered," dated it for 1995, and carried it in his wallet to stay motivated? It might sound odd, but what's amazing about this is that in 1995, he was paid exactly $10 million for his role in *Dumb & Dumber*! And the best part . . . he credits constant visualization with getting him there.

He's not the only one. Lindsey Vonn, one of the most successful Olympic skiers in history, has said her mental practice gives her a competitive advantage on the course. "I always visualize the run before I do it. By the time I get to the start gate, I've run that race one hundred times already in my head, picturing how I'll take the turns." Lindsey visualized the moves that would take her to the finish line.

These athletes, actors, and influential people started with a blank canvas. They dreamed up a vision of what they wanted for their lives, they believed it was possible, and they took action to make it happen.

WHAT'S THE COST?

Sometimes our goals and visions feel too big. Some days you might feel like they are unachievable or so far from where you are right now.

You can't do everything you want. But you can do anything that you have the passion to chase after. Most people don't follow their dreams. They realize what their dreams are too late and look back on their lives, longing for what could have been. You don't have to wait to be thirty years in a job you hate or ninety years old to feel that way.

Before I started my business, I felt the same. I was thirty-three years old, working a nine-to-five job with benefits. At the time, I had two young kids and was running an art business on the side. I enjoyed my nine-to-five job, but it wasn't what I was passionate about. It paid the bills and gave our family financial security. But it was demanding. I worked long hours, including running events on weekends. I was working what felt like the equivalent of three roles in one, and at my lowest point, I started experiencing face numbness and heart palpitations while sitting at my desk.

I was placed on a heart monitor for two weeks. Thankfully, this ticker is strong and nothing was wrong with my heart. But I was burned out. My adrenals were shot, my stress levels were high, and I was emotionally and mentally drained. I knew my heart wasn't in this job and when I eventually left, they hired three people to take over what I had been doing.

I tell this story because I've heard this time and time again from many entrepreneurs considering leaving or who have left the nine-to-five. We stay in positions or do work we don't love because it's "comfortable." It checks the boxes and helps you afford your life. But at what cost?

What is the cost of doing something you don't feel aligned with? What is the cost of putting your energy toward something you aren't passionate about? What is the cost of doing what you "should" do versus what you want to do?

The cost is *time*. And time is something we can't get back.

IF IT WERE EASY, EVERYONE WOULD DO IT

It's hard work to follow your passion. Life will throw you curveballs, knock you down in the dirt. It will make you question your strength and whether your passion is really your passion at all.

But if you devote yourself to your dream, to feeling successful—whatever that looks like for you—and break it down into achievable tasks, you will be one step closer to it.

In my business, I have the honor of working with many business owners, CEOs, and industry leaders, and the difference I see between those who are successful and those who aren't is *focus, discipline,* and *passion.* And at the core of this is *belief.*

Henry Ford was on to something when he said, "Whether you think you can or think you can't, you're right."

It's so important to get focused on your goals, to feel the reality of your dreams, to break your vision down into achievable tasks, to discipline yourself, to stop procrastinating because of fear or uncertainty. To just do it.

Every billion starts with a dollar. Every achievement starts with a vision and the belief that you will succeed. One step forward is all you need.

PLASTIC BEADS

I remember watching the plastic slowly start to melt, anxiously waiting to remove the heat so I could see my beautiful creation.

Do you remember crafting with plastic beads? You would carefully drop the colorful beads into place on the hard molds, see your design start to form, and apply heat with a hot iron (and parental guidance, of course) to bind the beads together to keep it forever.

As you start to make progress in your business, it's a bit like plastic bead crafting. You need to understand the big picture. Have a vision of what you are going to create and then use the outline and the guide to show you how to get there.

Sure, you can start to drop beads anywhere you want and it can still look nice. But when you have a plan in place and know exactly what you want your design to look like, you'll carefully and intentionally lay each piece right where it belongs, and thereby create something with ease and speed.

You can still follow your intuition, deciding to change the pattern or colors as you go, but ultimately you are following the core design. As you get pulled into the zone of creation, you might need to reference back to that guide every now and then to keep you on the right track. Then when the heat is applied and you're under pressure, instead of melting away and spilling over the edges, your hard work and intentionally laid pieces will mold together into a beautiful masterpiece.

MINDSET MATTERS

Mindset matters. It matters to your success, your resiliency, and your potential. It determines whether you believe in the possibility of your vision, it connects you to your why and the mission behind what you do, and it allows you to tap into your potential by having a process to succeed.

I grew up in competitive dance. I traveled a half hour to my studio seven days a week, practicing for four hours a day, from the time I was ten until I was seventeen. It was my second home. My work. My purpose. My routine. I remember one class in particular; we were training for a big competition and the words *I can't* came out of my mouth. My coach turned and said, "There is no such thing as *I can't*. There is only *I won't*." This moment stuck with me and sticks with me to this day.

My determination and drive come from a place where *I can't* is not an option. There is only *I will* or *I won't*. When you see the power in that, your world and the words you say to yourself change.

The key here is that you hold the power. You have the ability to choose whether you can or whether you won't. Your mindset matters. Your words matter . . . especially the ones you tell yourself.

> **GOLD** *nugget* — The most important words are the ones you tell yourself.

OVERCOMING FEAR

Georgia O'Keeffe is one of my favorite artists, a real force in this world whose influence has gone far beyond the stretches of the canvas.

She once said, "I've always been absolutely terrified every single moment of my life and I've never let it stop me from doing a single thing I wanted to do." When asked about her art, she said, "I always felt I was walking on the edge of a knife. On this knife I might fall off on either side. But I'd walk it again."

How many of us fail to do what we dream of doing because of fear?

Fear of being vulnerable?
Fear of failure?
Fear of the unknown?
Fear of fear?

But what's worse than living in fear is *not* walking the edge of what you really want to be doing in this life. Sure, you might fall off, but you also might stand strong and eventually fly.

Home fun

VISION BOARD

Sometimes on the way to your dream, you get lost and find a better one.

Lisa Hammond

When I was traveling home from Italy on a backpacking trip with my three kids, we stopped in an airport shop. I was grabbing snacks for the flight home when a little white porcelain dish caught my eye. It was in the shape of a cloud edged with gold, and on it read the Lisa Hammond quote I've included above. This dish sits on my bathroom sink to this day and reminds me to always look to the clouds, give shape to my vision, and dream without limits.

I invite you to dream big and create a vision board without limits. Whether it's on Pinterest or cutting and pasting magazine images, make the space, explore, and dream big!

Sometimes when we give ourselves the time and space to explore and play, we can find ourselves getting lost in our dreams. But getting lost can be useful, because we can end up discovering an even better dream.

KNOW IT

Sometimes we need to break down before we can break through.

Amanda Wilson-Ciocci

Did you know that through the process of metamorphosis, a caterpillar breaks down every cell in its body, turning to a pile of goo before transforming into a butterfly?

Have you ever had moments so low you wondered what in the world was going to pick you back out of the hole you were in? I've found myself in that hole a few times in my life and each time I have emerged as something new.

When I started this business, it was out of necessity. Just two months before officially launching it, I was released from my so-called steady nine-to-five without warning and felt like I had been thrown into a black hole. To say it was a shock would be an understatement. On top of that, my partner and I had just decided to move house. Because my job had been a remote position, we had made the decision only a few weeks prior to pack up our business in our hometown, sell our family home, and move our three children two hours north to a new town by Georgian Bay.

Georgian Bay called to my bones, whispered in my ear and lit up my soul. But it was still risky to pack up our entire lives and move somewhere new.

After getting over the initial shock, I scrambled to put my CV together and line up some interviews. We had a new, bigger mortgage and three mouths to feed, so there wasn't time to waste. I was confident in my skills—I had over twenty years' experience working behind-the-scenes, running businesses and launches in finance, corporate, education, and entrepreneurship. The thing was, I knew no one in this new town! And every job I'd had previously I had gotten because I knew someone who could vouch for my work and was able to get me a position.

Here I found myself in uncharted waters. I knew no one, had no local connections, and had to rely on fewer than five pages to adequately relay what it was I could do and how I could help.

In just two weeks, I lined up three interviews. The first interview went well . . . in my mind, at least. You know when you're 100-percent sure you've got it and then realize you don't, and are left feeling confused and questioning your intuition? Yup, it was one of those. After the interview, the company responded, "You're overqualified for this role. While we would love to hire you, we're afraid you'll get bored quickly, and what we need is someone who will stay in the role long term."

The next interview said something similar. Now it was all down to my third and final interview. I went into it confident in my skills, but knowing this was my last shot before heading to the local Starbucks to apply for a position.

I always say, if I wasn't doing what I was doing now, I'd be just as happy working at Starbucks . . . at least for a little bit, anyways. They are always so friendly and kind, even to someone who rarely goes (me!) and doesn't get their ordering system. *Can I have a double-double tall grande decaf latte that tastes like caramel but isn't too sweet?* When the look of confusion crosses their face, I know I've done it wrong. They politely get out the cup sizes, asking which one I would like and confirming that it is the caramel decaf cafe latte. It's a system, and one I'm not familiar with, but I'm learning. Each time I go, I have more confidence in my ordering process. I'll come back to that analogy later, but for now, back to the final interview.

It was shortly after my third and final interview that I hit my lowest point. After thirty minutes, the business owner said, "I would love to hire you, but you're overqualified for this role. I feel like I should be working for you!" I politely thanked them for their time, left with a smile, and went straight to the grocery store. I remember walking down the bread aisle and breaking down crying, wondering how I was going to feed my children.

When your mind is in a panic, it's hard to not think of the worst-case scenario, and it's even harder to dream. How do you imagine anything other than the mud you are stuck in? How do you see a way out when you feel stuck?

I drove home from the grocery store, sat in the driveway of our new home, and called my mom. I remember telling her about the interviews. I could hear the panic in my voice from not seeing what the road ahead or the detour around the bend would bring. And in a moment of silence and tears, she asked, "Honey, you have all these skills and years of experience . . . Why don't you start your own thing?"

LIGHT BULB MOMENT!

When you're a grasshopper in the weeds, jumping from blade to blade, it's hard to see where you are and where you need to go to cross the meadow. Sure, you get snippets of your surroundings as you launch off each blade, but then gravity takes you right back down again. Your only option is hopping among the grasses to make your way through. What you need to be is a bird, to soar above the meadow and chart the way through it. If you can't be a bird, then you need another pair of loving eyes to soar above for you, see where you are, and show you the possibilities that are within your reach.

On that call with my mom, she was my soaring bird, sharing her wisdom and turning on my light bulb moment. A spark ignited inside of me—I hung up that call with my mom and knew exactly what I was going to do.

That night I leaped into action. I set up a website using a free template on Weebly. I put every service I could possibly provide on those three pages and was ready to launch. Did I know how to build a website? Nope. Was I clear on my offers? Heck no! Did I know who my ideal client was? Sort of. Did I care? Nope. I needed work and was going into full-blown action mode to make it happen.

This is the great thing about having a vision. Once you are clear on where you want to go, the steps to get there instantly become clearer.

> **GOLD** nugget — Be a bird; soar above to see where you are and where you need to go to get through.

I remember the day of my launch so well. I was sitting in my newly converted garage office on a sunny day in May, feeling a cool, dank draft whisper along the concrete floor.

(Side note: Did you know that some of the world's most famous companies started in a garage? Disney, Microsoft, Apple, Dell, Virgin, Amazon, Google, and Harley-Davidson, to name a few!)

I was thinking that the only thing holding me back from launching my business out into the world was a name! As entrepreneurs, we will often find some reason to delay launching. Whether it's fear of being seen, fear of rejection, or fear of failure, we tend to find something to hold us back from doing the thing that both excites and scares us. And while that's been true for me, too, it wasn't this time. I really just needed a name to link up my domain and send it out into the world!

But this was my baby, something of my very own. And just like birthing my own babies, the pressure of picking a name felt immense. Would it suit the business I planned? Would it accurately describe all of what I had to offer? What are the name's origins and meaning?

What if it gets made fun of? What if I don't pick a good name, what if everyone rejects me after I build this, what if I fail . . . Okay, maybe they *were* fears about launching!

I remember feeling so frustrated that a name was the only thing holding me back. I called Kiel into the garage and said, "Can you *please* help me figure out what the name of this business is called?" And it was in the next moment that he pointed outside the garage window to a beautiful creature flying so delicately by and said, "Look! A *monarch*!" And I knew.

That day The Monarch & Co. was born! I launched the site, sent an email to all twenty of my email contacts (all family and friends), and started promoting my skills to the world. One week later, I had my first client. Four weeks later, I was fully booked with five clients.

WHY DID YOU START THIS ONE?

As entrepreneurs and business owners, we often have a range of skills. We wear many hats, allowing us to be successful in different ways. If you're a solopreneur, especially, you wear all the hats— you're the sales team, strategist, marketer, copywriter, designer, admin, and coach. Knowing and being this can be a lot.

As a business owner, *you* started *this* business. Knowing why you started this business over another one is *so* important. The answer is your compass, your anchor, your motivator, and your gold nugget!

> **GOLD** nugget — Why did you start this business over any other one? The answer is your gold nugget!

I started this business instead of any other one because I am crazy passionate about helping entrepreneurs discover, build, and launch their dream businesses. From big-picture visions to nitty-gritty details, I love helping you get organized and focused, so you can feel in control of your life and your business. I love seeing your vision and using my knowledge and experience to design an optimized and authentic route for you to move forward. I love, too, that I can simplify your life by helping you achieve your dreams. And I'm really friggin' good at it!

What are you really good at? What do you love doing? What are your unique and authentic gifts? What have you come here to do?

I started this business to inspire other women to do the same. To take risks, to believe in yourself, to build connections with your community, and to make a positive impact on the world around you while doing what you are uniquely meant to do.

I started this business for the butterfly effect—to make small, positive changes that ripple out into the world and make it a better place.

IF YOUR WHY ISN'T BIG ENOUGH . . .

Just because you can own a business it doesn't mean you should.

I will always tell you what you need to hear . . . even if it's not always what you *want* to hear.

There are some people who, through Deep Dive & Roadmap sessions, have realized it's not the best fit to be a business owner.

Natalie was one such client. She came to me with an idea. She dreamed of leaving her nine-to-five and running her own business. As we dove deeper and deeper during her session, truths bubbled to the surface. She discovered that she didn't actually want to run a business. She wasn't interested in leading a company or managing a team (even if it was only her to start). She definitely didn't want to market her services and had no interest in sales. It turned out that she really wanted better boundaries at work and what she really needed was a vacation. After the call, Natalie left with her road map, put in a request for paid time off, and established new boundaries at work, which allowed her to resume the role she loved working for a company she was passionate about.

> GOLD nugget — You don't have to own a business to make an impact.

Entrepreneurship isn't the easy route. Looking back, getting a paycheck every two weeks, with benefits to boot, was easy. But my heart . . . It wasn't in it. And I had a burning desire to do my own thing, be my own boss, become the leader I wanted to see in this world, and design a life that truly lit me up.

Owning your own business requires you to do the heavy lifting. You have to steer the ship, bring new business through the door, have impeccable customer service, and deliver consistently amazing results. You have to be forward-looking and internally driven. You have to think of the big picture and all the smaller tasks to make that machine work. So, if your heart isn't in it, if the why behind what you are doing and building isn't big enough, it will be hard . . . I'd even argue, almost impossible.

But if your why is big enough and you crave the life of entrepreneurship, it doesn't have to be hard. You just need a plan, clarity, and belief to get you through.

WHAT DO YOU WANT?

One of the questions I ask my coaching clients in their Deep Dive & Roadmap session is: what do you want? It's a simple question, but there is often confusion after I ask it. The question, though rather simple, feels big because it isn't specific. It's not *What do you want to wear today? What do you want to do this afternoon?*

Or *What would you like to eat for dinner tonight?*

The question I'm asking is simply, *What do you want?* What's the first thing that bubbles up to the surface when you hear that question? Try it. Get quiet for a moment, take a deep breath in, and ask yourself, *What do I want?* And without your mind getting in the way, what's the first thing you think?

When I ask clients this question in our sessions, I often hear:

- ✓ *I want freedom.*
- ✓ *I want freedom of time.*
- ✓ *I want freedom of money.*
- ✓ *I want to make a bigger impact.*

But the gold nugget of this and where the truth and clarity lie is: *why* these are important to you. Why do you need more freedom? Why does more time and money matter? Why is it important to you to make a bigger impact?

The answer to these questions is the why that lies beneath the surface. This is the why that will be your compass and is at the core of what you do. This is your "core why."

> **GOLD** *nugget* — Your core why will be your motivator.

It will be the thing you come back to in those hard times and the thing that propels you forward. This question is *so* important to the bigger picture and will help to motivate all the nitty-gritty.

CORE WHY

Another one of the questions I ask my coaching clients during their session is: What's your biggest why? What keeps you up at night? What motivates you on those low days and drives you toward something bigger and better? What's the thing that gives you goose-bumps and makes your arm hair stand up in excitement when you think about why you are doing the work you are doing? And why is that important to you?

This question is another one that isn't as straightforward as you might think. It was only after completing an exercise with my own coach that I discovered my core why. I'll share it with you here in hopes of you finding yours.

First, ask yourself why you started this kind of business instead of any other kind. Then ask yourself why that's important to you seven times over. When you get to the seventh layer—"peeling back the onion," as my publisher says—you reach your core why.

Here is how I used this process when I began thinking about writing this book:

1. Why is that important to you?

I want to create something that will inspire business owners to live up to their full potential and say yes to building a life and business they love. I want to use this book to elevate my business to the next level, diversify my business portfolio, and position myself as an expert in the field of business and launching.

2. Why is that important to you?

Because I know the feeling of empowerment that comes when you can create something successful from nothing and I want other women to experience that.

3. Why is that important to you?

Because we live in a world where women are not often empowered to live lives of their own design.

4. Why is that important to you?

Because I want to change that story.

5. Why is that important to you?

Because of Giulia, Luca, and Koen—my children, the next generation!

6. Why is that important to you?

I want to create a legacy and improve the world for my children and future generations.

7. Why is that important to you?

So they can feel empowered to live their best life and continue the butterfly effect.

My core why is . . .

The butterfly effect: small changes can make a big, positive impact over time.

Simon Sinek says it best: "People don't buy WHAT you do, they buy WHY you do it." When you know your why, you know how to effectively communicate with your audience and you will have a cohesive brand. Know who you are and what you stand for, and you will know how to reach your ideal clients so you can better serve them and make a bigger impact.

GOLD *nugget* — People connect with people and with story. Know your why, share your story, and connect with your ideal people!

MOTIVATION FROM AN ELEVEN-YEAR-OLD

One day I was sitting with my eleven-year-old for lunch, not feeling at all motivated to get the finishing touches of my launch assets ready for the week. I would go so far as to say I was having a bit of a pity party over my to-do list.

In his wise, eleven-year-old-soul words, he said, "I think I have something to motivate you, Mama . . . If you don't do this now, then you might not make as big of an impact this week, and then you won't be able to reach the people you know need your help, and then *they* won't be able to reach and impact the people that need *their* help."

To which I replied, "Thank you, Koen. You are one of my biggest motivators. I love your heart. I'll see you at dinner."

The butterfly effect is my core why. We make big and small decisions every day. From what to wear in the morning and whether to drink coffee or tea, to choosing business names and what it is we want for our lives going forward, our decisions have an impact. Even the smallest changes can make the biggest difference. But to come to that realization, I needed to break my vision open in order to find my breakthrough.

Hometun
CORE WHY

Work through seven layers of why to get at your core why. Once you have your core why, post it in your office, on your mirror to see in the morning, or in a favorite journal. A place which will serve as a visual reminder for why you are doing what you are doing.

BE IT

Flowers don't open and close according to who is walking by. They open and show their beauty regardless.

Rebecca Campbell

WHO YOU CAME HERE TO BE

Do you know who you came here to be? Do you get glimpses of her walking by a mirror or reflected in those around you? Do you hear her whisper in quiet moments and speak to your soul, lighting you up?

Visions often arrive in my dreams. Visions of the past, glimpses of the future. Little whispers that ask me to pay attention. I know when I have a vivid dream it's something I need to pay attention to—my intuition on this has never been wrong.

One night, after one such vivid dream, I heard a whisper, reached for a pen and paper, and wrote this:

A butterfly once came and whispered . . .

Something so soft, I almost missed it.

She whispered . . .

"Do you remember who you are?"

When I turned to respond, I only saw my reflection.

WHAT'S YOUR MISSION?

My mission in life is not merely to survive, but to thrive; and to do so with some passion, some compassion, some humor, and some style.

Maya Angelou

As business owners, we have a responsibility to show up and an opportunity to make a difference. Getting clarity on our mission and values is how we can start to create an impact. If you aren't clear on what your vision is, what your driving force is, or who you are and want to be in this world, then it will feel muddy. You will feel stuck and won't know what the right next step is.

GOLD *nugget* — Getting clarity on your mission and values is how you start to create an impact.

The backbone of the Canadian economy owes its strength in part to its entrepreneurs, after all.

Currently, there are more than 360,000 self-employed women in Canada, which is a 30-percent increase in women-owned businesses in the last ten years. Yet only 16 percent of Canadian small- and medium-sized businesses are owned by women.

I'm on a mission to improve this number . . . not just in Canada, but in our global economy.

By 2019, women-owned businesses in the United States were almost 13 million in number, exhibiting an impressive rate of growth over the course of five years' time. As of 2021, 31 percent of small businesses or franchises were owned by women.

The Women Entrepreneurship Knowledge Hub's *The State of Women's Entrepreneurship in Canada 2021* reports that "[i]n the face of the unprecedented challenges of 2020, Canadian women played a leading role in the creation and management of new businesses, pivoted to generate new jobs, and innovated in response to the COVID-19 pandemic."

My mission is to positively impact this world by helping women in business have the tools, resources, and support they need to build and launch the life and business they dream of.

The world needs women in business. It needs leaders who have a holistic approach to business and life. It needs you to step into who you came here to be.

BUSINESS OWNERS DON'T CRY . . . OR DO THEY?

Sometimes my clients are hesitant to talk about their emotional or personal experiences. I notice this especially in our Deep Dive & Roadmap sessions, where I am helping them organize and focus on growth. They often apologize when their emotions or tears come up during our conversation, thinking their feelings might not have a place in a business strategy session.

Sometimes we forget we are human. We try to compartmentalize our experience, removing the personal element from business planning to remain disconnected from the outcomes. No good will come of this.

Think of your business as a human body. Now think about giving that body a workout. (Whenever I visualize this, I focus on the legs, because mine, despite owning a standing desk, are often sitting at a 90° angle for most of the workday.) When you focus on strengthening one area of the body, say the area that feels weak or needs extra love and care, you inevitably neglect another area. For your body, your business, to function successfully as a whole, you need to consider and be aware of all its moving parts.

The thing is, businesses are run by humans, and we are affected by our physical and emotional well-being. If we ignore emotion in business, if we ignore what drives, motivates, or fuels us, then we neglect this part of our whole selves. As a result, our bodies and business will need constant adjustments and repair. They might even seize!

I'm sure you've heard it before: *Don't mix business and emotion. Think like a boss. Forget your gut, what do the numbers say? Leave your emotions at the door. Lead with your head, not your heart.*

We have been advised to remove emotion, the human element of an experience. Thankfully, those ideas of old are changing. In life and business, everything is connected. Everything influences and affects who you *are* in your business.

Instead, lead with your heart *and* think like a boss. Pay attention to your gut *and* look at what the numbers say. Be aware, take care of all the moving parts *and* serve from a place of integrity and honesty. Keep the big picture (the whole body) in mind *and* take care of all the nitty-gritty details (the moving parts) so it runs smoothly.

The next time you question whether emotion has a place in business, think of your core why and your mission. Think about who you want to *be* in this world and what inspired you to start this journey in the first place.

> GOLD *nugget* — You are what is unique about your business. You are what is unique about your story. Lean into it!

BE THE LEADER YOU WANT TO SEE IN THIS WORLD

As a business owner, you have so many chances to get it wrong. You are going to come up against situations that will challenge you, whether it involves client and customer management, employee or contract management . . . heck, even self-management—you are your own boss, right?

This presents you with an opportunity to be the leader you want to see in this world.

In over twenty years of work experience, I've had great leaders, bosses, and mentors. And I've had horrible ones, too. Ones who didn't have the skills or tools to create a business with both the head and heart. Ones who thought like a boss at the expense of others, favoring the bottom line over integrity and kindness. And while I could go into juicy details about those horrible bosses, I'd rather focus on the good ones, so you have something positive to focus on and model.

What I will tell you about those negative experiences, however, is that they held hidden gifts and insights that have strengthened my leadership skills as much as the positive ones have.

Let me explain with the following examples.

Once, I was told by a corporate employer that I wouldn't advance as fast as my male counterparts because I was a woman and might get pregnant and leave, which meant the company didn't want to invest in me. Knowing what I know now, I could have gone to HR with that one, but it taught me a few things . . .

GOLD *nuggets*

- Women are brilliant and amazing and should have equal rights in the workplace. We should not be devalued for what our bodies are capable of (which we may or may not use based on our choice alone) and should have opportunities to advance and succeed.
- Let your anger fuel your drive to make this world a better place. It's one of the reasons that, of a team of twelve (at the time of writing this book) at The Monarch & Co., eleven are women!
- Create a company culture that you want to be part of and that values *all* people.

Another time, I went to a meeting expecting a raise for all the work and growth we had seen in the company, but I was let go without warning and without pay.

GOLD *nuggets*

- Expect the unexpected!
- Always have an emergency fund.
- Lead with empathy, compassion and kindness.

I met one of the best leaders I've ever had when I worked as an executive assistant at a university. He was kind, compassionate, and advocated for my rights, even when I didn't speak up for myself. He created a team who loved working for him, his vision, and his mission. One of his sayings I always appreciated was, *This isn't brain surgery*. Meaning: while our work is important, no one is in a life-or-death situation. If we did the best we could today, whatever didn't get done would be here waiting for us tomorrow.

It's something we as entrepreneurs need to take note of. There's always something to do, one more email to send, a spreadsheet to update, and a strategy to improve. But we created our businesses to be present, to live the life we want to create.

Great leaders and mentors in my life have gifted me with these additional lessons, which I want to pass on to you:

GOLD *nuggets*

- Listen; the wisest person in the room is the one with their ears and eyes open and their mouth shut.
- Lead with compassion, integrity, honesty and kindness.
- Lead with your head and your heart.
- Hire slow, fire fast.
- Don't be in the habit of collecting red flags.
- Follow your intuition and trust your gut.

SHE NEEDED A HERO SO SHE HAD TO BECOME ONE

When I lost my stable job, I was the main income-earner for our family of five and suddenly I wasn't going to have a paycheck in my account in two weeks. No warning, no heads-up, and with not much in savings, what felt like no options.

I was in a new town, had bought a new house, and knew no one. The thought of returning to another nine-to-five was soul-crushing and would still not pay enough to afford our expenses. I knew if there were no other options, I could go back, and would if I had to, but every ounce of me was fighting that path.

When I started building this business, I needed clarity to successfully launch it into the world. I needed to know that it would be a business that would make money for my family, do something I was passionate about and feel connected to, and allow me to make the positive impact I wanted, with the freedom to choose what that looked like.

I had worked so hard to get where I was and now it felt like I was starting from the beginning. I needed a hero, so I became my own.

I created the business I needed for myself. One that I knew would help others just like me to find clarity on their path, purpose in their work, a positive impact on others around them, and the freedom they crave and deserve.

Now I'm a generating Gemini with sacral authority building a heart-centered business to change the world. I use my head to get clear on strategy, my gut to sense out how I feel about a situation, my heart to know when to lean in, and my intuition always.

EVERYTHING YOU NEED IS WITHIN YOU

Remember when I asked if you had ever experienced moments so low you wondered what in the world was going to pick you back out of the hole you were in?

I found myself in one of those dark holes both literally and figuratively in April 2006. An ultrasound and biopsy found cancer in my thyroid and we had chosen to move into my in-laws' basement while I was in treatment for a year. Just weeks after I underwent surgery to remove it, I found myself reflecting on this time in my life . . .

In the dark hole of a basement, a fresh wound across my neck, healing from something I feared would kill me. Lying in darkness, feeling deeper than the depths of the basement, the light felt out of reach. In the stillness, I heard a voice in the distance. Something that sounded familiar, maybe even my own. It spoke louder and said, "You are the only one who can get yourself out of here."

In that moment, I healed my spirit and found my power. Even in our darkest moments, we are never alone. I didn't need someone to save me and pull me from the dark hole; I needed to see what I needed to heal inside myself and bring out the light that was always within me.

GOLD *nugget* | When you see your power and realize your potential, you can be anything. Everything you need is within you.

TRUST YOURSELF

I was getting our house ready to sell. I wanted a big, bold, beautiful deep blue as an accent wall in the kitchen. I got all the tools and supplies ready to go, brush in hand, paint mixed, and I hesitated to start. I realized I hadn't taped the wall or the white cupboards to protect them from this big, bold blue.

I had stopped taping a long time ago, because I knew my steady hand could get the job done without it. But because I hadn't painted in a while, I hesitated and questioned whether I still could. With this limiting belief showing up loud and proud, I hopped down off the chair, spent time taping up the cupboards and wall, and then got to work painting. When the paint was dry, I pulled the tape off, only to find that it looked like my fingernails when I used to let my child paint them: all smudges, irregular lines, and tape tears. It was basically a bit of a hot mess!

Frustrated, I scraped the paint off where it shouldn't have been, got my brush back out, and fixed the lines *without* tape this time. If I had only trusted myself, I would have saved an hour of work!

Sometimes we hesitate. Sometimes we doubt our abilities. But the real magic comes when you trust yourself.

You are here with your business for a reason. You have knowledge, tools, and resources you can share with the world. You just need to lean in, *be*, and trust yourself. If you can't yet, there are always tools and resources out there to help you get the job done. Just make sure you use the ones that work for *you*! Otherwise, you'll be wasting time and getting frustrated along the way, scraping smudges and fixing errors you never needed to make.

> **GOLD** *nugget* — The real magic happens when you lean in, *be*, and trust yourself.

WE CANNOT BECOME WHAT WE WANT BY REMAINING WHAT WE ARE

Muscles need to break before they can strengthen. Caterpillars break down into goo before they turn into butterflies. Sometimes you need to break down or break open before you can grow.

One of my students told me that my process had broken them open in ways they never knew existed. Because of this, they knew there was no stopping them now.

Growth can be uncomfortable. I know it can feel overwhelming physically, emotionally, and mentally. But on the other side of that pain and overwhelm is where you are longing to be! Don't let the pain of growth slow you down or keep you feeling stuck.

> **GOLD** *nugget*
>
> Growth is uncomfortable. As B.K.S. Iyenger says, "Do not think of yourself as a small, compressed, suffering thing. Think of yourself as graceful and expanding, no matter how unlikely it may seem at the time."

In life and in business, we cannot become what we want by remaining what we are. When you lean into who you are meant to BE in this world and take consistent, focused action to get there, beautiful transformations are possible!

BELIEF

Do you know what stops you from reaching your goals?

Most people assume it's a lack of opportunity, knowledge acquired, education invested in. But all of these are wrong!

The single biggest reason that stops people from reaching their goals is *belief*! Belief that you can. Belief that you are worthy and capable of receiving great things. Belief that you can reach your goals and do what you set out to do.

One of my favorite artists, Bob Ross, says it best: "Talent is a pursued interest. Anything you are willing to practice you can do. The first step to accomplish anything is to believe you can do it. And I believe you can do it. Create a vision in your mind and believe you can do it. If you believe strong enough, anything is possible."

What you choose to believe about yourself matters. It will hold you back or propel you forward. When you bust through limiting beliefs, you set yourself up for some serious success—in your mind, body, life, and business.

> GOLD *nugget*
>
> The single biggest reason that stops people from reaching their goals is *belief*! What you choose to believe about yourself matters. It will hold you back or propel you forward.

When you hear the voice inside your head that says you can't, or that you're not good enough, or that you don't know enough, or asks who are you to do this, that this is too hard . . . reverse the script. Be the hero—reframe and rewire those messages:

- *I will do this.*
- *I am really great at what I do.*
- *I am worthy and deserving of health, wealth, and joy.*
- *I am wildly capable and intelligent.*
- *I am successful, powerful, and respected in my field.*
- *I love knowing that life is easy and fun.*

What limiting beliefs come up regularly for you? Think of one right now and write down the opposite.

I am . . .

CORE VALUES

Core values are a set of guiding principles that influence the way you make decisions, how you view the world, and guide both your personal and professional behavior. Your core values explain who you are at the deepest level, so when you have clarity about your values and align your life with them, you are free to be you!

After doing a values exercise with a wonderful colleague, Dr. Paula Moore, I discovered our core values at The Monarch & Co. The process was enlightening and made me feel more connected with my business than ever before.

Knowing your values, both personally and professionally, are key to growth and alignment. Here at The Monarch & Co., they are:

1. **Quality:** We have high expectations of ourselves and aim to always lead with and deliver quality to the clients who trust us with their businesses.

2. **Connection:** Entrepreneurship can be a lonely road, but together we can do beautiful things and create a world where people are connected to their purpose and their passions.

3. **Integrity:** We do what we say and say what we do, and always with a heart-centered perspective.

4. **Impact:** This is something we like to call the butterfly effect. 🦋 Helping good people do good things and make a bigger and better impact on this world.

5. **Gratitude:** We feel it for the team we get to work with, for the clients we have the honor to work for, and for this wild, crazy, beautiful journey.

6. **Fun:** Because who doesn't want more fun?

> GOLD *nugget*
>
> When you start aligning your life with your core values, the people, clients, customers, and collaborators start to align with you. They start leading you in your decisions, resulting in a purposeful and aligned life.

Homefun

CORE VALUES

While the values exercise I did with Dr. Moore was an extensive deep dive that I highly recommend, this Homefun is a simple exercise to help you determine your core values and start aligning your life and business to them. Write down what you believe your five core values are below.

Head to the Additional Resources for a fuller, more detailed exercise. Once you're done, come back to the values on this page to see if they align.

My core values are . . .

1.

2.

3.

4.

5.

GIVE IT

Everyone is not your customer.

Seth Godin

It's a common belief that when we start our business, we need to reach as many people as possible. We love what we do, we believe everyone will benefit from our services, and we want to help as many people as possible.

These are all good things, but you are also probably familiar with the phrase that if you speak to everyone, you speak to no one. It's so important to really understand who you are speaking to, who you are helping, who you want to help, and how.

When you know *exactly* who you serve, it becomes so much easier to speak directly to them. When you get specific on who they are, it means you know their needs and pain points inside out, and therefore you can pinpoint the areas where they need the most help and support. You know where they are now, you can see and feel the muck they are stuck in, and you know how to get them to where they want to be. By giving them what they need, you give your business the best way to succeed.

In this chapter, we are going to work on getting to know your ideal clients on a deeper level. If you've done this before and don't think you need to do it again, you're mistaken! As you and your business grow and change, so do your ideal clients. Any opportunity you can take to get to know your clients and customers better is an opportunity for you to better understand and serve them.

> GOLD *nugget* — It's not one and done! Any chance to get to know your ideal clients on a deeper level is an opportunity for you to better understand and serve them.

To do this, we will look at niching down, serving your audience better with lead magnets while simultaneously serving your business by building an email list, and most importantly, doing some market research that will connect you with your ideal clients and get you excited about your offers!

I SEE IT ALL THE TIME

Clients come to me with perfectly packaged, *amazing* courses, memberships, programs, and offers that provide unbelievable value, solve major issues . . . and that no one buys.

The problem isn't usually the product. It's that it wasn't the right offer to the right audience at the right time. Part of this equation is understanding *who* your customer is.

It's so important to get clear on *who* you are serving with your business and your offers, *where* they are hanging out so that you can reach them, and *what* their biggest challenges are so you can help them.

These questions will help you get clear on your ideal client avatar so you can better inform your decisions, offers, and marketing.

GOLD *nugget*

Just because you have an ideal client avatar doesn't mean you can't serve other client avatars. It just means you are *super* clear about who you can best serve and connect with.

QUESTIONS ABOUT YOUR IDEAL CLIENT AVATAR

I want to challenge you to get super specific. As heart-centered entrepreneurs, we often think about *all* the clients we could possibly help, hesitant to close the door on anyone who might benefit from our services. But as you answer the following questions, I want you to think of just *one* client. Either think of the most ideal client you have ever had or one that you would *love* to work with.

- Who are they (age, pronouns)?
- What is their profession? Are they working nine-to-five in a corporate position they hate or are they their own boss?
- How do they feel at the end of the day? Are they frustrated, overwhelmed, tired, and feeling stuck? Or are they happy, excited, driven, and calm?
- What are they passionate about?
- What is their biggest challenge right now?
- What are their common pain points (no money, no time, lack of clarity, fear of failure)?
- What are they afraid of?
- If they could snap their fingers (Mary Poppins–style) and have the life they wanted right now, what would they be doing?
- What is the most important thing to them and why?
- What do they need the most right now?
- How does it make them feel to envision themselves succeeding at their goals?
- What will succeeding at their goals do for their life and for their family?
- Why is that important to them?

I read an inspiring book when I was first building this business which changed the course of my own business. In *The Pumpkin Plan* by Mike Michalowicz, he asks, "If you could bring one client to a desert island, who would you bring? Who could you be with for months, who can you trust, who do you love, who might actually work with you to find the way out to survive or even thrive during your stay?"

GOLD *nugget* The answers to these questions will illuminate your ideal clients. These are the clients you want to work for and build your business around.

You are a visionary and entrepreneur! Since you have the ability to choose what you do and who you work with and for, I have two questions I need you to answer:

Who do you want to work with? And why is that important to you?

I want to work with . . .

It's important to me because ...

Once you have answered these questions, you're ready to write up a client profile for your ideal client avatar. This is a one-page summary describing your ideal client in *incredible* detail. Before you start writing, though, there's one thing to consider before you do this ...

THE RICHES ARE IN THE NICHES

One of the hardest things for heart-centered entrepreneurs to do is niche down. We want to help everyone and the thought of getting super specific about who you can help and how you help them can feel limiting and counterintuitive.

But to have a successful and thriving business where you are connecting with your ideal clients and your ideal clients are connecting with you, you must be super specific with who they are and how you help them.

First, it's important to distinguish between your *niche market* (who you are helping) and your *niche product* (the product or offer you are selling to help them). You can niche down your market without niching down your products. This is where knowing your ideal client and where they are in their journey is key, because you can assist with products and offers that will best help them.

Because this can be such a challenge, here are some simple steps, using a yoga teacher as an example, to help you identify your niche market. Consider:

1. Who all the potential customers are in your industry:
   All people who practice yoga
2. Who you can serve in this industry:
   Everyone who practices yoga in my town
3. Who you are most excited to serve:
   Yoga practitioners who have at least 200 hours of yoga teacher training
4. What your niche is, given your previous answers:
   Yoga mentor for yoga teachers in training in my town

Now use your niche market to determine what your niche products or offers would be. Our yoga teacher's niche products might be:

- *Yoga teacher training for beginners*
- *Yoga teacher training for intermediate practitioners*
- *Yoga teacher training for advanced practitioners*

When you've narrowed down your niche market, you can create a "how you help" statement, which you can use just about anywhere. Here's one using the yoga teacher example:

> *I help yoga teachers in training deepen their yoga practice through mentorship so they can better support and serve their yoga students.*

MARKET RESEARCH

Once you have your niche market, it's time for market research! This is often a step that gets skipped because we get too excited about our offers.

Please, for the love of your life and business, do *not* skip this step! I've seen many entrepreneurs build incredible offers packed with so much value that no one buys because they didn't do the market research to validate the offer before they built it. They hadn't made sure what they were building was something their audience wanted and needed.

In your Homefun for this chapter, you'll be invited to do some market research and dive into learning more about how you can best serve your ideal clients by discovering what it is they truly want and need. That is, if you don't make the following mistake.

THE BIGGEST MISTAKE

Your biggest mistake is not listening to your customers. When you're building a business and launching new offers, you need to know what your customers need and want from you. You need to know what problem you solve, why customers value your business, and why they purchase from you.

My papa always said, "The wisest person in the room is the one with their eyes and ears open and their mouth shut."

As an entrepreneur and business owner, your first job is to *listen* and *watch*, then act. Too many business owners do the opposite; they build and create based on what everyone else is doing and then hope what they've created resonates and sells. But doing it in this order means you've missed the most important step.

I learned this the hard way when I launched my first digital course. I "knew" what my audience needed and spent three months putting together a course I "knew" would help them. Ten modules and 300 video minutes later, I had a finished product. I launched the program and was met with less-than-overwhelming results. A few students had bought and completed the course, but they weren't seeing the results I had hoped for. I didn't understand—I had poured so much value into this, so why wasn't anyone seeing the transformations I had anticipated?

I did what I should have done before I created the course and went back to the drawing board. I asked my audience what they needed. Turns out, they didn't want another course that they would buy and then park on a list of "courses to get through one day." They wanted to learn from me directly. They trusted my coaching, loved real-time accountability and feedback, and didn't want to watch videos to gain access to me.

I listened to my audience, looked for the gold in their feedback, and changed the structure of the course based on that information. To this day, my signature program, Monarch Business Academy, morphs and changes based on feedback I get from students, so that I can better serve them and they can experience better results. Just like marketing research, it's not one and done. If you want to build a better business, you need to *be* a better business! And that means listening, changing, and adapting to what your customers want and need.

GOLD *nugget* — Ask for what your customers need and want. Ask them what problems they need solutions to. Ask them why they value your business and purchase from you. Then *listen*, take notes, and take action to help your audience solve their problems. Be a wise business owner and you will be here long after the loud ones have gone.

HOW DO I REACH MY IDEAL CLIENTS?

This is one of *the* most common questions I get asked. It's the worst feeling as a business owner to know you have an amazing product or service, fully understand and know who your ideal client is, and then not know how to reach them. Or worse, try to reach them and hear nothing but crickets when you do.

The first and most important step to reaching your ideal clients is to be really clear about who they are. You need to know *exactly* who you are speaking to. So if you've skipped the Ideal Client Avatar exercise before this, this is your gentle reminder to do the foundational work before you move on. Once you do, then it's time to share my secret sauce for client communication!

My secret sauce is like any great Italian recipe, in that it has three ingredients:

1. **Consistency:** Consistently showing up and providing value where your ideal client is already hanging out. If you're not visible to your ideal client, you have a problem.
2. **Story:** Remember, people connect with people and your story matters. Share your story, and you will connect with your ideal client.

3. **Sharing:** Share how it is you help your clients. Get super specific about it. If you want to reach people and grow your audience and business, you have to be willing to put yourself out there and engage.

GIVE IT

Audience- and list-building, regardless of your niche or industry, need to be the top priorities of your business. While the followers you gain on social platforms are nice to have, you don't own those platforms. You *do* own your email list. While the algorithms and rules change for each platform, your email list remains the steadfast constant.

In my signature program, Monarch Business Academy, list-building is one of the first things we do. In fact, I tell my students, if there is *one* thing you take away from the program, it's this: your list and clients are the biggest assets in your business. And this holds true for both brick-and-mortar and online businesses.

We saw this highlighted so painfully at the start of the pandemic in 2020. Businesses with an online presence who prioritized their list easily pivoted their focus entirely online and were able to stay connected to their clients and customers. Those who didn't either had a big learning curve ahead of them or lost clients and business.

Again, you don't own the social platforms where you've created accounts. Your email list is not affected by a platform's rules and algorithms, which makes it your best asset in your business. This is made incredibly clear with Sarah's story.

Sarah, a Monarch Business Academy student, was launching a signature offer and products to her audience. During the launch, Sarah's Instagram account was hacked by scammers and suddenly frozen by the platform. It took almost two weeks and multiple verification methods for Sarah to get her account back, all while she was launching over a busy holiday season! If Sarah had only focused on growing her business on Instagram and relying on her followers there, her launch and sales would have been wildly disappointing. Instead, most of Sarah's followers were also email subscribers, so she still had access to her customers and her launch was a success.

> **GOLD** *nugget* — Your list is the biggest asset in your business. If you want to build a successful business, you need to prioritize and focus on list-building.

HOW DO I BUILD MY LIST?

There are lots of ways to build your list, with launching being the very best way. We'll get to that in a later chapter, but for now, let's look at some easy ways you can start building your list today!

One of the easiest and quickest ways to build your email list is with a lead magnet. A lead magnet, sometimes also referred to as a freebie or an opt-in, is an integral marketing tool for your online business. It is a (usually) free resource that you promote to your subscribers in exchange for their email addresses. This is a powerful way of marketing, because your ideal client is giving you permission to land in their inbox, a sacred space which should be respected.

The great thing about creating great lead magnets is that it creates an exchange: it provides value to your ideal client by solving their problems or challenges while at the same time, helps to build their knowledge of, like for, and trust in you.

LEAD MAGNET IDEAS

Great lead magnets solve problems! They can help your ideal clients save time and money, reduce overwhelm, or even transform mindset.

There are lots of different ways for you to create your own lead magnets. I've popped some here to get the creative juices flowing:

- **Quizzes:** A quiz is a great way to find out more about your audience and segment your subscribers! Quizzes are top-performing ways to increase your email list, but they can be extensive to build.

- **Video Series, Webinars, Master Classes, or Work-shops:** This could be a live three-day training or a five-day challenge—something that shows your expertise and builds a connection with your audience.
- **Email Funnel Training:** This training is provided over multiple emails over a period of time (for example, five to seven daily emails trickling out information on a specific topic that addresses your audience's main struggle).
- **Templates, Guides, Checklists, or E-books:** These are usually between one to fifteen pages and should be something your audience would be willing to pay for.

> GOLD *nugget*
>
> The key with lead magnets is to provide actionable wins or takeaways that your audience can apply right away to experience real transformation.

KEY FEATURES OF LEAD MAGNETS

When you are building your lead magnets, there are key features you should include to ensure you see results:

1. **An Amazing Headline:** You want to capture the attention of your audience.
   a. Weaker: *Things you can do to help reduce your pain and feel better in your day.*

      b. Stronger: 3 *Easy Tips to Reduce Low Back Pain Now*

2. **A Subtitle:** This is a short sentence letting your audience know what's in it for them.

      a. *These three easy tips will immediately reduce your low back pain, strengthen your core, and create freedom in your body.*

3. **First Name and Email Fields:** Make sure this section is compliant with the latest data privacy legislation. This often involves including small print that explains how and why you will be using the information they submit.

4. **A Button:** It's always best to go for clarity over catchiness with button labels, but adding your personality can be a fun way to connect with your audience. So instead of *Subscribe Now*, you could do something like *I need this in my life now!*

5. **A Welcome Sequence:** This is a warm welcome you make to your community through an email sequence. I explain this in more detail in the next section.

Once your lead magnet is created, it's time to shout about it from the rooftops! With so many options these days for promoting your business and offers, here are a few ways you can share yours:

- **Your website:** As a pop-up in the top fold of your home page.

- **Social platforms:** Instagram, Facebook, Pinterest, YouTube, TikTok, LinkedIn, etc.
- **Collaborations:** Master classes, podcasts, interviews, media, etc.

If you have spent the time, market research, and energy to create this resource, make sure you also spend the time and energy to share it. Just because you build it, doesn't mean they will come. You need to show and share it!

WELCOME TO THE COCOON!

I love a good warm welcome! When friends come over, I make sure to greet each guest with a hug at the door, invite them inside, offer them a refreshing drink, and ask about their day. A welcome sequence in your business should do the same!

A welcome sequence is the email sequence linked to your lead magnet. It's the introduction to your community and a way for you to build a sense of know-like-trust with your audience.

Your welcome sequence can be as short as one email or as long as fifteen, but the sweet spot is usually around three to five emails in length.

GOLD *nugget* — The sweet spot for a welcome sequence is three to five emails. Start with your end goal in mind and work backward from there.

Email marketing is something we go in depth about in MBA and it should be something you put at the top of your to-do list. For our purposes here, let's go over the structure of a five-part email sequence:

Email #1: *The Delivery Email:* Thank your new subscriber for signing up and provide a direct link to the freebie.

Email #2: *Introduction to You & Your Biz:* Share a story of how you got here—remember that people connect with the why behind what you do.

Email #3: *The Challenge:* Share some common objections and frustrations.

Email #4: *The Solution:* Bust through those objections and frustrations by sharing testimonials or social proof.

Email #5: *Offer to Solve a Problem:* Introduce your product or service, or with an invitation to join.

NOW WHAT?

Okay, you've created your lead magnet, promoted it on your social platform, and subscribers have joined and moved through your welcome sequence . . . now what?

You are going to consistently send value-driven emails to continue building know-like-trust with your new subscribers. This might not be the flashy fix you wanted, but in business, consistency is key.

So many entrepreneurs don't want to send emails because they feel like they are bothering their audience. They don't want to be "that annoying business owner" or feel pushy or sales-y. The best advice I can give you here is, don't! Don't be pushy or sales-y, don't be the business owner that just writes an email because you "should."

Instead, write because you want to help. Write because you want to connect and build relationships and community. Be consistent. Put value into building relationships with your community. And one of the best ways you can do that is through your email marketing.

This is how you share through story and connect person-to-person. This is how you can show transformation and provide value to your audience. This is how you can help your subscribers solve problems, show them you are the bridge from where they are now to where they want to be, and build authentic relationships with them.

You don't have to write novels every week to connect with your audience. In fact, I recommend you don't!

Many subscribers are skimmers! So break up the text, use **bold** for important sections, address your subscriber by their name, and write for them!

Don't write for your list, write for your ideal client—because when you speak to everyone, you speak to no one.

When you start to build your list, you want to also be building connection and engagement with your subscribers. Make them feel welcome, just as you would a guest in your home. I love to include a call to action (CTA) in every email to inspire engagement. These can be simple prompts, like *Download this new resource I know you'd love, Join me for a free master class here, Reply and let me know your thoughts, Book a call, Buy now*, etc.

And for the love of your list, don't ignore your postscript (the section after your sign-off). This part of the email is read the most often. Here you can summarize your email in one sentence and include a CTA.

Building a community takes time, it takes consistent effort, and it takes heart. If you don't love what you're doing and who you're doing it for, your audience will feel it and it will affect your growth.

GOLD *nugget* — Consistency is key. Consistently invest in your community, create content to help your ideal client, and show up because you want to help.

Homefun
MARKET RESEARCH

Market research is an important component of your business strategy and a tool used to gather information about your ideal client. We dive deep into market research inside MBA, going over the different types and when to use them. The best market research is done 1:1, but here are some other ways you can easily gain valuable information about your ideal clients:

- ✓ **Have 1:1 Conversations with Your Ideal Client:** These conversations can be done by phone, email, or in person, and will give you insights into their world, which is key to finding out what they need. When you have these conversations, you want to ask open questions. Your main job is to listen, *not* pitch or provide solutions. If I wanted to find out more information about my launch clients, I would ask questions like:

  - Could you tell me a story about the last time you launched?
  - What was the hardest part about that?
  - Why was that hard?
  - Why is that important to you?

> GOLD *nugget*
>
> When conducting market research, your job is to listen, *not* pitch or provide solutions. You are looking for the gold nuggets that will help you serve better.

✓ **Survey Your Audience:** You don't have to create extensive questionnaires to gain valuable information from your ideal clients. Create Instagram polls, ask questions in emails, or send out a short Google Form.

✓ **Research Competitors**: Looking at businesses that have similar offers to yours is a great way to gather data and market research. You can read the comments and questions their clients ask in order to find the gaps, common themes, and struggles they share with your ideal client. Then you can see how you can help your ideal clients solve those problems.

> GOLD *nugget*
>
> Remember that market research isn't something you do once and it's done. Your clients' and customers' needs are always growing and changing, just as you are. The more you research, the more you understand your clients, the better able you are to serve them, and the more your business succeeds.

BUILD IT

Rome wasn't built in a day, and neither should your business.

Amanda Wilson-Ciocci

I was in complete awe on my first visit to Rome. Every step I took had me marveling at what was in front of me. I had known that this city was beautiful, but *this* beautiful?

What is it about Rome that gives it such incredible beauty? You've likely heard the expression before that *Rome wasn't built in a day*. This city has thousands of years of history, art, and culture stacked on top of each other. Seeing these layers of time, I knew I was witnessing the slow process of striving for greatness. The city keeps investing in the best so it can be its best. This didn't happen overnight. It has taken millennia, and the evidence still stands today.

When it comes to your business, you want to build it so it lasts, too. Think of putting a roof on a rocky structure—it's likely to fall in and injure someone. So, as you build your business, don't cut corners or take the easy way out. Strive for excellence. Take your time finding the best method and tools you'll need to build a strong foundation and don't be afraid to invest.

In this chapter, we will look at building a strong foundation, things to consider as you build, and the goods on what you need to launch online, as well as how to structure, price, and sell your signature offers.

As you read on, ask yourself: What kind of business are you building? Are you building to create long-term, Rome-like awe, or are you thinking short term?

THIS WASN'T MY FIRST BUSINESS

Fun fact . . . The Monarch & Co. isn't my first business! I've had a few in the past—I sold lemonade on my childhood street, embroidered bracelets for friends, and at the risk of dating myself, upsold one-cent candy at recess in grade school.

My first real business started when I was just eighteen years old.

My high school sweetheart (now husband) and I started a catering business. We were called KIAM Catering (*KI* for Kiel and *AM* for Amanda). Our family came up with the name and it's stuck ever since! We catered private parties, wedding engagements, retirement parties, and anniversaries. I had barely any skills in the kitchen, but Kiel was training with a professional chef, so I was there to prepare food, serve, and clean up, Marie Kondo–style. (I friggin' love cleaning. It truly sparks joy for me!)

My second real business—you know, the legit kind, where business cards were printed and a website was built—I started when I was twenty years old. It was called Raven's Wisdom and I intuitively channeled for private clients. I had clients from across the country booking calls every week to have sessions with me to learn the wisdom I channeled from my spirit guide.

The third business, KIAM Studio, was another collaboration, but which has stood the tests of time. It's a business where Kiel and I create mixed-media paintings, bringing our styles together on one canvas to create work that focuses on collaboration, connection, slowing down, and looking intensely at the world around us. We started it in 2010, the year my first son was born, and we continue to create commissions for private collectors.

Shortly before my third child was born in 2017—and by shortly, I mean three days—we opened a secondary business called Art

In The Ward. It was a beautiful art studio, with high ceilings and exposed brick walls, in the heart of our town. It was a space other artists could use for shows, photo shoots, and creative events. We hosted paint nights, art fundraisers, private events, and collective shows for the art community, operating for two years before passing the space over to our mentees to take over when we packed up our life and moved to a new town in 2019.

Aside from my official businesses, I also dabbled in wedding and event planning and freelance photography before officially starting The Monarch & Co. I have a creative mind and an open soul, and I'm eager to learn and help impact this world in a beautiful way.

I started this business in 2019 out of necessity, but every day since, I build it with intention, passion, and a vision of the effect it is having on the world. I am building for excellence, for sustainability, and for impact. Just like Rome, I want clients, customers, and our team members to be awed by its beauty and feel the love that is poured into it.

> GOLD *nugget* — Find your creative spark. Follow your passions, love what you do, and create a life you get excited about.

WHAT DOES TOILET PAPER HAVE TO DO WITH YOUR BUSINESS?

(Not that business, your actual business.)

When the pandemic started in 2020, my town, along with many others, was eagerly stockpiling toilet paper.

I remember a call with my sister, who said, "I've got my Costco-sized package. Did you stock up?" And I said, "Nope. We've been buying rice, flour, and some canned goods, because if this goes crazy, you can't eat your toilet paper!"

While everyone was going overboard, purchasing toilet paper for twenty dollars a package on Amazon, I ordered my family a hand bidet. TMI? Yup, but if you've been to Europe or practically any other place on the planet outside North America, having one is standard bathroom practice. It's amazing and everyone should have one. So, instead of panicking about toilet paper like everyone else, I knew we would be more than okay with our hand bidet if the world ran out of toilet paper.

While you might be questioning your book-buying choice at this moment, stick with me and let me explain what this has to do with your business.

While everyone is zagging, you should be zigging. Watch the zagging: study the competitors, research the market, look for gaps . . . and from that, find opportunities to zig, to do something different. Something sustainable, useful, valuable, and wanted.

> GOLD *nugget* — Do things differently—zig when everyone else zags.

This is the wonderful thing about building your own business. You get to choose. With that being said, what will it be for your business . . . toilet paper or a bidet?

MAKE YOUR MONEY WORK FOR YOU

As you build your business, every dollar you spend on it should make you money. Save to invest, not just to save. Make your money work for you and the possibilities available to you will only be as limited as your beliefs.

As a small-business owner, here are some of the ways you can start to make your money work for you:

- **Reinvest your profits to improve systems.** This is the "roof and plumbing" of your business. From the outside, there haven't been any major changes or fancy upgrades, but on the inside, you're not sitting with a metaphorical bucket to catch leaks or unclogging old pipes. Reliable systems will set you free in your business.

- **Market to bring in new leads.** Digital marketing is a necessity for small businesses. It can be done relatively cheaply through your social media channels or with joint venture partnerships. An important note, which we will dive into shortly when we cover low-value activities, is to not assume that because you are doing the work, there is no cost. When you manage your social media, for example, it might not cost you as much money as hiring a social media manager, but it is costing you time. And time is your most precious resource!

- **Invest in your team.** Get one, if you are wearing all the hats and haven't already. Contract out your low-value activities so you can focus on the growth of the business. Spend time working *on* the business, not just *in* it.

- **Invest in you.** Get a mentor or coach who has been there before and can show you the optimized route to success. Investing in myself and my business has been the best money I've spent. When you work with a coach who can help you with mindset and strategy, it will decrease time spent and you'll be able to focus on getting your important work out into the world.

> **GOLD** *nugget* — Every dollar you spend in your business should make you money. Save to invest, not just to save.

OVERNIGHT SUCCESS

Athletes don't hope to win . . . they train. Singers don't dream of singing . . . they practice. You can't bake a delicious cake without all the ingredients. So don't expect to have a successful launch and business if you don't put in the work.

Success doesn't come overnight. There isn't an *Easy* button you press to receive your dream life. It takes time, dedication, passion, and all the ingredients needed to build a successful business and launch working together.

The first female self-made millionaire in the United States of America was Madam C.J. Walker. An African American entrepreneur and philanthropist, she was tenacious, remarkable, passionate, authentic, and driven. In her own words, she said, "I had to make my own living and my own opportunity. But I made it! Don't sit down and wait for opportunities to come. Get up and make them."

Hoping, dreaming, and believing *are* key ingredients, but so are strategizing, optimizing, and action. Rushing to bake a cake isn't going to make the cake any faster. You have to wait for the oven to preheat and the ingredients to combine; then patiently, you have to wait for that cake to rise, hoping that you haven't missed a step, so that when you open the oven door, you'll find a perfectly fluffy cake waiting for you to enjoy. When you have the right ingredients together in the right proportions, under the right conditions, you have a recipe for success. But don't rush the process. Every good recipe takes time, patience, and love to create.

A WORD ABOUT ONLINE BUSINESS

I had a great conversation with a student who was launching an online coaching business and was feeling a little overwhelmed by *all* the things she needed to know and understand when running a business online.

Years ago, she ran a brick-and-mortar business. "It was so different," she told me. "Those were the days of ads in the local paper, flyers in people's mailboxes, fall registration shows or trade shows, and open houses. I built my business on word of mouth and kick-ass classes. Once people met me in person and experienced a class, they were sold."

Gold nugget time!

> **GOLD** *nugget* — Online business is not different from the "good old days" of marketing. Our mailboxes are now our inboxes, in-person workshops and shows are webinars and master classes, and word of mouth will always be your best business.

The difference in the online space is *impact*. Your potential to reach more people is much larger but the fundamentals are the same. Connect with people where they are, solve a problem, and help guide people on their journeys. You don't have to do all the things. But when you build a strong foundation, come with a true intent to serve, and a passion to make a difference, everything else in this space becomes easier.

As you build, keep these aims in mind: focus, low-value activities, and profit. I'll expand on each briefly.

FOCUS

When everything is important, nothing is important. Regardless of the size of your to-do list and projects, look at your week ahead and plan to succeed. Ask yourself, if nothing else were to get done this week, what are the five big things that need to happen to move the business forward and spark joy?

LOW-VALUE ACTIVITIES

I know this may sound silly, but my vision is too big for my body. The vision I have and the things I want to accomplish with my business are too great to accomplish alone. If I want my vision to become reality, I will need the support of others to see it through.

When you are running a business, there are always a lot of moving parts. You may be the CEO, operations manager, admin, bookkeeper, graphic designer, communications support, and marketer all in one day. Add on being a parent, partner, friend—oh, and don't forget the self-care—and your day starts to feel *real* full.

So, what's the answer?

Lighten the load. Organize. Prioritize. Focus. Invest. Adopt the mindset that if you have a big vision, you will need support to help you get there. Be the visionary of your business and invest in a team to make your dream a reality. By delegating or outsourcing your low-value activities instead of getting bogged down in their nitty-gritty details, you stay in your genius zone and build the vision you dream of.

Your genius zone is the sweet spot in your work. The spot where your strengths, talents, and skills overlap. When you're working in your genius zone, things feel easy and like they're in flow. You'll know you're in this zone when you are excited about the work you are doing, time seems to fly by, and you are contributing to the growth of your business.

Low-value activities like responding to emails and inquiries, scheduling meetings, and updating spreadsheets are necessary and important. But as a business owner, you want to focus on the high-value activities or "needle-movers": the ones that contribute to the growth and success of the business.

To determine your low-value activities, you calculate your hourly rate. Numbers don't lie. I will give an example below, using a whole number to make things easy. What you want to do when calculating your low-value activities is this:

1. Take your yearly salary. (This can be a forecast if you haven't been in business for a full year. In this case, you would take one month and multiply by twelve.)
2. Divide your yearly salary by the number of weeks in the year.
3. Divide that number by the number of hours you work in a week.
4. The result is your hourly rate.

    For example, let's say your yearly salary is $100,000. You divide that amount by 52 weeks and then divide again by 30 hours a week, which results in $64.10 per hour.

Now let's say you have administrative tasks in your business that are not in your genius zone, take you a long time to do, and could be contracted out at $30 per hour. Anything that costs less than your personal hourly rate to complete is a low-value activity and should be outsourced so you can spend time on higher-value activities that contribute to the growth of your business.

To determine exactly what your low-value activities are, write a list of all the tasks you do in your business for one week. Once you have all the tasks written down, categorize them in three ways: activities you love and want to keep (high-value activities); the tasks that take you a long time to complete and suck the life from you (low-value activities); and finally, the activities you want to remove, automate, or create a system for.

This is a great exercise to do on a quarterly basis because it's so easy to fall into old patterns and get busy in the weeds.

GOLD *nugget* — Audit your business tasks regularly and stay focused on your high-value activities as much as you can. Doing so will help you save time and build a successful business that sparks joy and drives profit.

PROFIT

Looking at your profit will help you determine what to keep and what to get rid of in your business. This is often the hardest thing to do for heart-centered entrepreneurs. You love all your offers and the ways in which they help your clients. But you need to make sure your offers also help you and the business.

To start, let's make sure we are on the same page about what I mean by profit. Gross profit is the simplest profitability metric because it defines profit as all income that remains after accounting for the cost of goods sold (which is how much it costs to make and deliver your service, offer, or product).

When I completed a deep dive into my profit margins just one year into my business, it was a game changer! I realized some of my offers weren't driving much profit and some I was actually paying to deliver! While it was a bit shocking to see the results, it was so important to know how to move the business forward.

The easiest way to determine your profit is to make a list of all the ways you make money in your business. Maybe you provide 1:1 hourly consulting, a passive digital product, and a coaching container. For each offer, you want to look at your estimates for the past twelve months and compare that to the revenue they generated, the profit margin percentage, the time it took you to deliver those offers, and whether each offer sparks joy for you (arguably the most important metric).

> **GOLD** *nugget* — All metrics are important. The magic comes when you can help your clients get results by doing what you love *and* driving profit.

Looking at the answers to these questions will help you determine which offers to keep and which to remove. Whichever ones you remove, use the time, money, and energy saved by doing so to provide your best value to, as Mike Michalowicz says in *The Pumpkin Plan*, "feed your prize-winning pumpkin."

Here we are . . . We've talked about toilet paper, making your money work for you, the illusion of overnight success, and the value of your time and focus. Next, we will get into the nitty-gritty of sharing what you need to launch online and how to structure, price, and sell your signature offer.

WHAT YOU NEED TO LAUNCH ONLINE

Regardless of where you are in your business and launch journey, there are tools you will need to set you up for success, save you time and money, and automate your life! What you need to launch online comes down to having a few simple systems in place.

1. **A Lead Magnet Creation Tool:** This is the free resource you are going to create and share with your audience to build and grow your email list. If you skipped over the last chapter where I covered this, go back. Building a list is relevant and necessary to every business. The type of lead magnet you create will determine the type of support you need. For example, if you are creating a freebie checklist, you are going to use something like Canva to help you create a branded design. If you are creating a free video training series, you can use software like Loom or Zoom to record it. For the budget-savvy biz owners,

using your computer's camera or your phone with a headset works great, too. The key to video recording is great lighting and sound quality.

2. **An Email Marketing Platform:** For list-building, audience connection, and funnel creation. Free services are great when you're starting out, but as you build your list and want to tag and segment your audience more dynamically, the paid versions are best.

3. **Payment Processing Software:** This is something like Stripe or PayPal. It's a way for your clients and customers to automatically purchase your offers.

As you build your business and launch your offers, the key is simplicity. Simple systems help you scale and keep you from feeling overwhelmed with all the things you have to do.

GOLD *nugget*   Keep it simple.

HOW TO STRUCTURE YOUR SIGNATURE OFFER

When developing your signature offer's framework, you want to start with the end result, then the journey you are inviting your students or clients to go through. Ask yourself, what is the one result your students will receive upon completing the journey?

If you're creating a coaching container, think about this in terms of coaching sessions. I remember helping one of my coaching clients to structure the three different coaching packages she offered: a one-month package, a three-month package, and a six-month package. Her three-month packages sold the most, but she was finding her clients needed more support by the three-month mark. Most would join on for another three months and see amazing results and transformations, while those who decided not to commit for another three months did not. She rarely sold the one-month packages, except to clients who weren't exactly ready to do the work. It was clear to her that the most significant transformations happened with the six-month package. But she was afraid to let go of the one- and three-month packages and only offer the one option.

Here's the thing: you started this business to help people. If you know the best results are going to come from a particular method or a given time frame, then that is what you need to provide to your clients. In MBA, we work through the Signature 8 Method, which consists of eight key steps to successfully build and launch a signature offer. If I stopped at the fifth step, you wouldn't have everything you needed to best support your business and launch, and you wouldn't see results.

To make this example even clearer, let's think about building a piece of IKEA furniture . . . the bane of my existence! Say I've ordered a desk and brought it home, excited to get it set up in my office. I've been working against propped-up pillows on my couch before this, and it's been doing some serious damage to my neck and lower back. I unbox the 30 smaller boxes, open the 50 bags of screws, and get out the full, 300-page manuscript of instructions. I start flipping through it, page by page, and working through the steps of building my new desk. By step 33 of 333, I can see the vision coming together and the desk starting to form, but it still looks like it might end up in the firepit if I don't pull this together soon. At this point, I flip to the next page, only to find there are no more steps. Instead, there is a message: *To continue building your dream desk, head to this link and purchase the remaining instructions.* A heat fills my face and the desk is suddenly one step closer to being firewood. Now I have a choice to make: Am I ready to make the investment and hope the next book will have the rest of the instructions I'll need to finish this desk? Or do I check out, deciding that pillows propped on the couch are working for me and the wood would be better used for fire? It *is* winter, and a fire would be nice! Sure, I might be doing some ergonomic damage with my current setup, but it's been working for me this far.

I think you get the idea. If you want to help your clients and customers experience the transformation they are looking for, you need to offer only what is going to best serve them. For my client, that means knowing the six-month package is all she needs to provide the results her audience is looking for.

Is there a specific journey you need to lead your customers and clients through that will show them results? Is there an ideal number of coaching sessions your clients should complete to ensure they reach their desired goal, end result, or transformation? Either way, you're thinking about the end result and the journey in order to determine the structure of your signature offer. In teaching, we call this backward design.

There are three main steps to creating your signature offer:

1. **The Brain Dump:** Make a list of all possible topics you will need to cover in the program. When brain-dumping, have no fewer than three and no more than fifteen topics. These topics should cover what your students must know in order to achieve transformation. You can ask yourself questions, like *What key concepts will students need to understand to achieve the end results? What key skills will students need to learn to achieve the end results?*

2. **Prioritization:** It's time to prioritize! Take your list and determine what the best order is to present the topics. Think about the desired end result here and work backward to prioritize the journey.

3. **Supporting Resources:** Once you have a framework in place, you will need to brain-dump all the supporting resources to go along with what you'll be teaching. These

can be Homefun-like activities to help them integrate their learning, case studies or testimonial examples, or bonus materials (like videos, PDFs, and additional readings).

Putting in the time to think about your students' journey is so important! Going through these steps will help you streamline their transformation by focusing on what is most important. At each phase of this design process, your focus should always be on the end result and how to best support your clients and students in order to achieve it.

Know where your clients are when they start a program, where their challenges and roadblocks will be along the way, and how you want to create change and transformation in their lives.

When you understand this journey and really understand your client, you can then insert some love along the way to make their experience a better one. For example, at Week 7 inside MBA, when students may be feeling overwhelmed, cracked open, and a little vulnerable, I like to make the cocoon cozy, welcoming, and a reaffirmation that they are exactly where they need to be.

Working backward from your desired outcome ensures the journey you create integrates all the learning they will need to reach that end result.

HOW TO PRICE ANY OFFER

Blindly throwing a number on your price tag will most likely leave you frustrated and not seeing the sales you want. Pricing can become a bottleneck for many businesses when launching their offers out into the world! But my goal in this section is to make sure that isn't the same for you.

Block out some time in your schedule (seriously, do it right now), grab a pen and paper, and start thoughtfully going through the following questions as you consider your signature offer. Going deep to really understand the why behind your price will help you sell your offers with confidence.

When you look at how to price your offer, keep these five points in mind:

1. VALUE

Consider the type of offer you are creating: a membership, course, product, service, 1:1 coaching, etc.

Once you have the type of offer you are creating, ask yourself these questions:

- ✓ What kind of value are you providing?
- ✓ If your client or customer implements what you are teaching or offering, what is the value to them?

✓ What is the return on their investment?

For example, Monarch Business Academy takes you through the Signature 8 Method, which teaches you everything you need to know to grow and scale online using different methods to launch. You can use the tools and resources of this single program again and again to not only launch, but to keep growing and scaling up online for as long as you are in business. The potential for implementing this program has massive ROI!

2. SUBTYPE

The second thing you will want to consider is the subtype of your offer. Is this a beta, beginner's, or signature offer?

- *Beta offers* typically use penetration pricing, where you offer the lowest price you feel comfortable with to get new clients, generate revenue, show you can get results, and gather testimonials, while at the same time, building your brand and reputation. This subtype incentivizes your audience because it's typically the first round of a new offer, which usually means lower pricing and greater support. Beta, get the best!

- *Beginner's programs* target beginners (of course) and as such, usually come with a lower price point (under $500).

- *Signature offers* command a higher price point because they contain high-value content and support ($500–$10,000).

The subtypes I have included above are trends, not rules. For example, it doesn't mean you can't have a beta program that runs for beginners with a price tag of $5,000. There are strategies for knowing how to price your offers and what the market will accept. Which leads me to my next point.

3. MARKET RESEARCH

Though it's key not to fall down the rabbit hole of market research or get distracted by what others are doing, completing some market research is important when pricing your offer. You'll want to look at similar businesses and their offers and ask yourself these questions:

- ✓ What are they doing?
- ✓ What are they offering?
- ✓ How are they pricing their offers, and what's included?
- ✓ What are their payment options?

Compare your offer to others and see where you want to be in the market. Do you want yours to be known as the cheapest, middle-of-the-road, or high-end premium?

Consider how your offer is different from others. You can evaluate these differences, adding monetary value to positives and subtracting negatives, to come up with a total for your offer.

For example, say your competitor's offer is priced at $4,000. In the table below, you compare each detail of the offers.

Offer Details	Their Offer	Your Offer	Value Difference ($)
1:1 Coaching	monthly	weekly	+ $1,500
Educational Modules	5	10	+ $500
Bonus Trainings	0	5	+ $500
Expert Guest Speakers	3	0	– $1,000
Online Community	yes	no	– $500
Total =			+ $1,000

Based on your comparison, your offer has a $1,000 value over your competitor's. Therefore, you can price your offer at $5,000.

As an artist, I relate this valuation to the art world. There are some collectors willing to pay $5,000 for a painting that others wouldn't pay $100 for. Some paintings are valued at $2 million where others are valued at $200. The difference comes down to a few factors— the experience of the artist, the art piece that is being valued, the market it's being sold in, and the buyer. All these factors play into how to price your offers and are something to be aware of when thinking about yours.

4. IDEAL CLIENT

Your ideal client is usually a few steps behind you in your business journey. Put yourself in their shoes. If you were them, would you buy your offer? What would they invest in? What would they believe would be worth the investment?

You have to know who your ideal client is and price your offer accordingly. What makes the most sense and what would they be willing or able to pay?

5. KNOW YOUR NUMBERS

The final important factor to consider when pricing are the costs of your offer. After you have determined the type of offer and completed some market research, you need to look at your numbers and determine what your profit margins are.

- ✓ **What is the cost of getting the lead?** (What does it cost you to bring in new leads to your offer? Are you running ads or do you have affiliate marketing payouts? How much time is spent creating and marketing your content? Are you promoting both online and in-person?)

- ✓ **What is the cost of fulfillment?** (This can vary depending on what your offer looks like. Perhaps you have an onboarding process that includes handwritten notes and curated gift boxes, for example. For completely automated and prerecorded evergreen offers, the costs of fulfillment are less, but would still include processing costs such as billing fees, taxes, etc.)

When pricing your offers, you want to look at *all* the numbers and make sure what you are charging makes sense. The cost to the customer needs to be higher than your costs to deliver and fulfill, otherwise you may end up doing what I did my first year—paying to deliver your offer every time you sell it!

GOLD *nugget* — There is *no* one-size-fits-all, no hard-and-fast rule to pricing your offers. You have to choose a price you feel comfortable with (one that both excites you and makes you nervous), will work for your business, and your ideal client will be willing to pay.

(If you're a coach, I have a guide to help you with pricing your offers. You can access it in the Additional Resources.)

SALES PAGES

Sales pages are *so* important to your launch. A great sales page will even make the sale for you! Make sure to spend time creating this page, ensuring you communicate the value of your offer and the incredible transformation that it can bring. I always recommend having a biz bestie review it for feedback before pushing it live.

Below are the key components to include on your sales page:

1. **Craft an Opening Headline:** The goal of your headline is to capture your ideal client's attention and keep them scrolling the page. You want your audience to read about your offer and what it can do for them. Focus on the main benefit of your offer here.

2. **Create a Picture of Your Audience:** Where is your ideal client in their life right now? Illuminate their pain points with empathy.

3. **Create a Better Image or Story:** What kind of a future do you want your ideal client to imagine for themselves? How will that make them feel?

4. **Present Your Opportunity:** Give an overview of your offer. Provide a visual mock-up or actual image of it.

5. **Introduce Yourself:** Include a photo of yourself. Make sure you talk about why you created your offer and how it's important to you. This is your time to position yourself as the expert and share your story. Be you, be real, be authentic.

6. **Explain Features & Benefits:** You can talk more about the features and benefits of your offer in this section, but keep it brief and valuable.

7. **Share Results & Testimonials:** Share how your offer will transform your audience's lives. Highlight testimonials or case studies.

8. **Show the Investment Required:** Tell your audience the actual cost value of investing in your offer. Adding more value than the actual cost is a great way to meet and exceed expectations, but don't make up numbers here. They must have a real value. Consider what each of the offers would cost if they were bought separately.

9. **Define Who This Offer Is For:** You want to attract your ideal customer and make sure they are investing in an offer that will be valuable to them. Setting clear expectations about who this offer is for and who it *isn't* for avoids frustrations, confusion, and refund processing. You can include this as a separate section or include it in the FAQ section.

10. **Include an FAQ Section:** Here is where you'll address the most common objections to buying, the time requirements for the program, your return policy, etc. Make this a drop-down feature to save space on the page and provide a reassuring guarantee to your readers.

11. **Add a Final Call to Action:** Ending with a quote is a lovely way to connect with your audience and inspire them to make a decision about your offer. In some ways, your sales page should conclude like a letter from a good friend. But remember to insert your final CTA button!

GOLD *nugget*

Start a folder in your Google Drive or on your computer with sales page samples you love! Make note of headlines that inspire you, images you connect with, and sales pages that are clear and concise. Come back to them for inspiration when you create your own!

Homefun
TASK AUDIT

This chapter is full of goodies that will impact the long-term success of your business. Start by doing an audit of all the tasks you are doing in your business so you can determine what your low-value activities are and come up with a plan to contract those out.

Then you can focus on the high-value activities: designing your signature offers, pricing your offers to best align you with your customers, and building a business to last.

GOLD *nugget* — Rome wasn't built in a day. Keep it simple and build for quality, sustainability, and impact.

REACH IT

Consistency is key. Success doesn't come from hoping things will work out. It comes from taking consistent, aligned action.

Amanda Wilson-Ciocci

In business, a huge part of your success is the strategy you use to get you to the next level. There are often eye rolls and resistance in my community of heart-centered business owners when I use the word *strategy*, but hear me out. Strategy is more than just tips and tricks and the latest marketing trends.

It's thinking about all the moving parts of your business—the offers, the customers, the big vision—and putting together a well-thought-out plan to achieve a major goal.

Without a crystal-clear strategy in place, every tactic and tool is a waste of your time, energy, and money. You won't get to where you want to go. How you combine the latest marketing trends, tips, and tricks with your creative skill to connect your audience to what you create and produce (and sell!) matters.

Regardless of where you are in your business, this chapter on strategy will be relevant. Tactics and tools will change, but strategy is forever!

In this chapter, we are going to look at how to reach your audience strategically and authentically, what to look out for and be aware of when you do, and how to ensure you are doing it in a way that works for you.

WHAT IS THE PURPOSE OF SOCIAL MEDIA?

Social media is an amazing tool for communication. So many people are on their devices scrolling the latest news, creeping their friends, and looking to solve problems online.

The thing to be aware of when incorporating social media into your marketing strategy is that social platforms are owned by other companies. The great thing about this is that the platform is already built and the audience is already there; your job is to connect with that audience, build your community, and deepen relationships.

The negative side to this is that another company determines the rules of the platform. If rules and algorithms change, you will need to change your strategy, too. If you don't, you risk being shut down or shadow banned (i.e., the platform will stop showing your content to your audience because you've stopped creating the type of content the algorithms want to see . . . you've broken the rules of their game).

For this reason, you want to consider social media only *part* of your strategy. What matters most is having a strong foundation to reach from. When using these platforms, create an authentic connection with your people but harness the traffic and audience to your email list (a space you own).

> GOLD *nugget*   Without harnessing it to a strong foundation, social media can be a waste of time, energy, and money.

BUILDING ON A BED OF SAND

One of the best metaphors I've heard about entrepreneurs and social media was from Jeff Walker when he said building a business on social media is like "building on a bed of sand." With rules and algorithms always changing, it can be overwhelming trying to stay ahead of the latest curve or trend. For this reason, I won't go into the tactics to use on different social media platforms, but I will address the overall strategy you should be thinking about when using social media as a marketing tool.

BE WHERE YOUR AUDIENCE IS

There are many social platforms out there and they are always changing! Facebook, Instagram, LinkedIn, Pinterest, Twitter, TikTok, YouTube . . . each platform has different rules of engagement and different ways to improve conversion and connections with your audience.

> **GOLD** *nugget* — The key is to be where your audience is.

Many online entrepreneurs use Facebook, Instagram, TikTok, Pinterest, and LinkedIn to connect with and build their audience, but you need to know which platform is right for you and your business. Regardless of what platform you use, it's *all* about consistency and connection.

Consistently show up and meet your audience where they are with an authentic representation of who you and your business are. Consistently provide solutions to your ideal client's problems. Consistently engage with your audience to build relationships.

BUILD YOUR BRAND

Social media platforms provide an opportunity for you to build your brand. By regularly publishing content, you position your business and call in your ideal clients. As your following increases, so will your social proof and authority.

GOLD *nugget* — Remember that followers are not subscribers. Use social platforms to connect with your audience and build your email list.

When you create a social profile online, spend some time on your bio. This is your opportunity to show people how you help your ideal clients and how they can connect with you.

A NOTE ABOUT CONSISTENCY AND COST

When it comes to strategy and posting on social platforms, do what you will be consistent with. If you can consistently make one post per week, then start there!

The key is to start with a strategy. If you don't have a strategic content plan, you will waste time, energy, and money. Here's where many entrepreneurs get it wrong: they think because they are doing their own social media management, it isn't costing them anything, when the opposite is true.

When you do your own social media marketing, you are planning the strategy, developing the copy, creating the graphics, researching hashtags . . . and that's before the content even makes it to the platform! Once you're on the platform, you have to publish your content, think about how to engage and connect with your audience, and spend time nurturing relationships. And if you aren't super-focused with your strategy, you are playing a game in a high-risk environment.

These social media companies have invested millions of dollars to keep users on their platforms. So while you may be spending time there strategically, posting and engaging for your business, you might also find yourself watching ten Good News Movement videos. Suddenly you've lost an hour of time. And as I mentioned before, time is your scarcest resource; it costs money to waste.

> **GOLD** *nugget* — Just because you run your own social media accounts doesn't mean you're saving on costs. Time is money and your scarcest resource.

The goal of your social media strategy is to build community, get to know your ideal clients better, and increase engagement. When you're launching a product or service, you will want to increase engagement leading up to your launch, but that doesn't mean ghosting your audience when you're not. If you don't show up regularly for your audience, how can you expect them to show up for and trust you?

Consistently say what you're going to do and then do it. Consistently show up and provide value to build know-like-trust—in banking terms, make more deposits than withdrawals. Consistently lay the foundation by reaching out to grow and connect with your people.

When I landed my first $30,000 coaching client, she first reached out to book a discovery call before signing with me. When I asked her where she heard about me, she told me she had been following me on Instagram for three months. She liked what I posted about, found my advice helpful, and noticed that I was consistent with my messaging and the value I provided. This client never engaged with my account, never voted on my Story polls, never wrote comments, never even liked my posts. She was simply there, watching to see if I did what I said *consistently*. Consistency is key. You never know who is watching, listening, and waiting to work with you!

> GOLD *nugget*
>
> Your network is your net worth. Consistently show up the way you want to be seen and build an authentic connection with your audience—it will create the impact you are looking to make in this world.

CONTENT PILLARS AND THEMES

Strategic content planning involves building your content pillars. These are the central themes of your business that you regularly speak to and focus on.

The sweet spot is four to six pillars that are content themes or buckets specific to your brand and most popular with your audience.

Every time you create content to publish, ask yourself:

✓ Is this what my ideal client needs to hear?

✓ Is this helpful to their lives?

✓ Does this inspire or help them in some way?

> **GOLD** *nugget* — A great content strategy can only be created when you truly know *who* your ideal client is.

A good content strategy drives multiple results. Of your four to six content pillars, some content should drive sales, some should drive website clicks, and some should inspire the audience to share. All of these play to the algorithms, the rules of the social media game. This is why varied content pillars and different types of posts (inspirational, educational, personal, entertaining, promotional, and social proof) are important.

✓ Plan your content and review it every ninety days.

✓ Check your analytics dashboard to see which type of content is performing well and what is resonating with your audience.

✓ If you're struggling for content ideas, look at some of your competitors for inspiration. What are they posting, and what are their ideal clients commenting and struggling with?

✓ Know what you want to achieve, create a plan, and stick to it.

Working backward from your goals, launch, or big vision is always the best plan. You need to know your destination to know which direction you need to take next.

FOLLOWERS ARE VANITY METRICS

Key Performance Indicators or KPIs tell you what content to lean into, what is resonating with your audience, and most importantly, what isn't! While there are many different metrics to track on your social media platforms, the key ones to look at are engagement and conversion rates.

Content that is saved by your audience is important to pay attention to. Saving it means it resonated enough with them that they want to come back to it or share it at a later date. Similarly, take note of content with the least engagement. If you are spending time and energy creating content that isn't resonating with your audience, then you are wasting valuable resources that could be redirected to content that is connecting and converting.

Although I know the world gets excited about followers (I've found myself doing the same), these are vanity metrics. Your followers are not the same as your subscribers. And while having lots of followers and an engaged list is important, what's more important is harnessing that traffic and converting your followers to subscribers on your email list.

> **GOLD** *nugget*
>
> Followers are not the same as subscribers. Harness your traffic on social media platforms to build your list with a lead magnet.

REACHING YOUR IDEAL CLIENTS

Assuming you know *who* your ideal client is and where they are hanging out (a detail often overlooked yet key to the next steps), here a few ways you can reach your ideal clients:

- **Host a live webinar or workshop.** Live webinars are the highest-converting forms of marketing to date!

> GOLD *nugget*
>
> Pack your live session full of value! Your audience's time is valuable, after all. One of the worst things is leaving a live workshop feeling like you haven't received anything valuable from attending, or worse, feeling like you lost an hour of your life you can't get back. Your webinars and workshops should solve the problems your ideal clients are facing right now with quick wins.

- **Partner up with a business.** Think about other companies that share your ideal client base and whether a collaboration could be mutually beneficial. Reach out to them!

> GOLD *nugget*
>
> Partnering with another business that complements your business is a great way to grow together! Hosting a joint webinar benefits both businesses and provides value to your audiences.

- **Appear on podcasts.** Pitch a discussion topic to five podcast hosts you feel would align with your business values and whose audience could benefit from your content.

> **GOLD** *nugget* ┼ Have a media kit ready for these kinds of opportunities.

I'm not going to lie: it takes consistency, dedication, and a big vision to continue showing up and giving value to your audience so you can build a successful business and bring in new leads. But when you do, your ideal clients are watching and waiting to work with you. Keep going, keep showing up, and do the work!

KEY THINGS TO KEEP IN MIND

As you reach out to your audience, there are a few key things to keep in mind:

🔑 Show up consistently where your ideal client is hanging out. If you're not visible to them, this is a problem—hope marketing is never a good strategy!

🔑 Lead with a strong brand identity and share your story (your why). As Simon Sinek says, "People don't buy what you do, they buy why you do it."

☞ Remember that riches are in the niches: First, niche down and get super specific about *what* you offer, *who* it is best fit for, and *how* you help, Then tell people what you offer and present your audience with the opportunity to transform with *your* product or service.

☞ Reach your audience by providing value (in the form of content, webinars, or offers, for example) and help your ideal client solve their problem.

In order to do all of the above effectively, you have to understand who your audience is, what motivates them, and what they need from you *right now* to solve their problems. When you unlock this key information, that's when you will really connect with your ideal clients and help them get from where they are now to where they want to be.

A WARNING ABOUT SOCIAL MEDIA AND LAUNCHING

Using social media is a great way to complement your launch and create bigger results for it. Just remember that you don't own the platform; rules and algorithms can change and this can affect access to your account or its reach at any time.

I've had students inside MBA, who, for various reasons, had their accounts shut down in the middle of a launch. It can be extremely stressful because it's part of your launch strategy and it feels like social media is the only place where you're engaging with your audience. But if this is true, you have a bigger problem. Social media should only be a component of the launch—your main launch results are going to come from your subscribers on your email list.

A typical launch conversion is 2 percent of your email list. Meaning: if you have an email list of one hundred people, you can expect that two of them will buy the offer you've launched. Not very exciting numbers, I know! But don't worry, there are many ways to improve this conversion rate. I've personally seen and executed launches with over 25 percent conversion rates or that earned $50,000 with an email list of one hundred subscribers. It is a lot of work, though, and there are multiple factors at play.

We will get into the structure of a launch in the next chapter, but remember to keep your social media strategy complementary. Focus the content you publish on building the momentum of your launch and with every action you take for your launch, mirror it on your social media.

A successful launch takes dedication, consistency, patience, and action. It takes having the right opportunity and using the right strategy, for the right people, at the right time. It also means knowing that you likely won't get all this right the first time.

Hometun

AUDIENCE ENGAGEMENT

It's time to reach your audience! Use the information from this chapter to engage your audience and start a conversation. Whether that's a poll on Instagram or an email to your list, ask them what their biggest struggle is with _____ (insert the problem you help them solve). You could ask what they would like to see more of from you, how you can better serve them, or if they could learn more about _____ (insert how you help), what would they want to know?

LAUNCH IT

The longer the runway, the better the takeoff!

Amanda Wilson—Circci

You made it! This is the chapter that makes me excited for you and for what you will launch out into this world. As I write this, I can see you in my mind, hopefully with a hard copy in your hands—because we all know flipping through book pages, feeling the texture of the paper, brings a certain weight and certainty with it, a weight and certainty I know you carry for the possibilities available to you. The weight of knowing you have a gift to share with the world and the certainty that you will launch it to those who need it most.

First, we needed to do the work to get here. We needed to go on a journey to gain the experience and knowledge that would get us to this point. After all, we're building Rome here, not a weekend carnival!

One of my favorite pieces of advice I share with my MBA students is: *The longer the runway, the better the takeoff!* As the daughter of an air traffic controller, you can see where I'd get the analogy. In business, we are always looking to collapse time, take the shortest route on the road map, and get the quickest fix for immediate results. And while there are times when all of that is possible, when it comes to launching, the longer your runway is, the better your takeoff will be.

Launching is one of the best things you can do for your business. It will grow your subscriber list, bring in new leads, and position you as an authority in your niche. If you didn't feel my love for launching before this chapter, you might just feel it beaming through the pages ahead.

In this chapter, we will cover what launching is, why it's important, who it's for, and what you can launch. We will dive into the five-phase launch and talk about your launch impact, the purpose of prelaunch, open cart, and the most important step of your launch. We will discuss why numbers are important, as well as reframing failure. This chapter's a juicy one (it could likely be another book), but let's dive in!

WHAT IS LAUNCHING?

I love to start here because entrepreneurs can either overcompli-
cate or oversimplify the launching process, and there is error in
doing either!

Launching, in its simplest form, is a systematic way to get your
product or offer out into the world. It is a strategic way of getting
the word out about your product or offer, and it's just as important
as the work involved in developing your business idea in the first
place.

So often, business owners focus on building their products and
services, but then put less effort into thinking about how to get their
work out there and, as a result, don't see the response they had
hoped for. My aim is to ensure you avoid these disappointments
and open you up to the possibilities available to your business.

> GOLD *nugget*   Launching is just as important as
> the development of your product or
> business idea.

WHY IS LAUNCHING IMPORTANT?

Launching is important because it is relevant to everyone who
owns a business!

I often get pushback here with business owners who say *I don't like to sell* or *I'm not really launching anything*. But the truth is, if you own a business, you are selling something. And if you are not selling something, you are not running a business . . . or at least, not a successful one!

> GOLD *nugget* — Launching is relevant to everyone who owns a business!

Launching is the opportunity to share your offers with the world. Just because you build it doesn't mean they will come. Your audience might not know about your offers, or that they even need them. Launching gives you an opportunity to share your work with your audience and shout about it from the rooftops!

Through the process of launching, you build a stronger connection with your audience, your impact increases, and you can reach more of your ideal clients. It's how you build your list, which is key to any business's success. All these benefits, and I haven't even mentioned that it also delivers a cash injection.

WHAT CAN YOU LAUNCH?

Now that we know what launching is and why launching is important, the next step is figuring out what to launch.

Lots of entrepreneurs love the idea of launching, but what holds them back is deciding what to launch. There are *so* many possible offers you could choose from, but to help spark some creative ideas and broaden your thinking, I've made a list of some excellent examples:

- 1:1 coaching
- services
- online information products (memberships)
- high-ticket offers (signature programs)
- e-commerce (physical products)
- events (on- and off-line)
- podcasts
- art
- books
- new offers in an existing business
- free lead magnets for list-building (e-book, PDF guide, checklist, master class, webinar)

YOUR LAUNCH IMPACT

In order to know if you're on the right track, you need to first acknowledge where you are and where you want to go. Before you head into a launch, you want to take the time to determine what you want the impact to be.

What is the goal or outcome of your launch? Is there a revenue goal? Is the goal to build your list? Are you selling a lower-ticket offer in the hopes of gaining a larger reach? Are you launching a new offer? Are you launching a product to lead your audience to another back-end product or offer? Who are you trying to reach with your launch? Why is it important to launch now? How will your launch's success be measured?

There are many reasons to launch; knowing what your goals are before you set out will help keep you focused along the way.

FIVE PHASES OF A LAUNCH

Launching is not just what happens on launch day or during launch week. Rome wasn't built in a day, your business wasn't built in a day, and neither should your launch be built in a day! Sure, the week your launch happens is the fun and energetic part, but it's not what it's *all* about. There are five phases to a successful launch that span a few months:

1. **Prework:** The phase in which you are laying the foundation, building your audience, doing market research, and validating your offer. This is usually three to six months before your launch.
2. **Prelaunch:** The prelaunch period is crucial to how successful your launch will be. It starts three to four weeks before you open cart and includes your prelaunch event (which we cover later in this chapter). During much of this time, you are talking about your offer and building momentum for your prelaunch event,

promoting it everywhere, and inviting your audience to join it. Remember to add everyone who joins your pre-launch event to a dedicated "launch list"—tagging and segmenting your audience in your email marketing is important and will make your life easier in the long run.

3. **Open Cart:** The period of time when your offer is available for purchase, lasting anywhere from twenty-four hours to seven days. I've had students and clients extend their open cart periods, with some lasting more than fifteen days, but I advise against it. The open cart period requires that you be forward-facing; your energy has to remain high and engaged. While that seems like an easy thing to do when you're excited about your offer, the combination of forward-facing activities, managing the nitty-gritty elements behind the scenes, and still having a life outside of your business makes a long open cart exhausting work. My advice is to start with the five- or seven-day sweet spot. Certain offers can remain available after the open cart period (an open membership, for example), but this period of time should be used to promote a specific offer or bonus for joining during this window of time. Doing this will bring attention to your business, get more eyes on your offers, and call in your ideal clients.

4. **Postlaunch & Launch Debrief:** Once you close your cart, several actions need to happen to maximize your

launch impact. Most immediately, you will want to create an onboarding sequence for your buyers and include any bonuses you promised during open cart. Gratitude is so important in this phase. You will also want to send out an email to the subscribers on your list who did not buy, thanking them for joining you on the launch journey and surveying them to ask why they didn't buy. This will help inform the most critical step of your launch: the launch debrief. Analyzing what worked, what didn't, and how it will affect what you'll do next time is crucial while it's still fresh in your mind. It's arguably the most important step, and when done right, gifts you with gold nuggets about your audience and information for your next launch.

5. **The Launch Effect:** Sometimes more negatively referred to as a "launch hangover," this is the postlaunch period of rest and recovery. You have just spent four weeks building excitement for your launch, focused outward—having conversations, delivering value, supporting new incoming business, *and* managing email sequences, inbox management, payment processing, and all the other nitty-gritty aspects of launching. It's important to take some time to rest and recharge, whatever that looks like for you. It could be a bath with no interruptions, a walk in nature, or a two-day silent retreat. Whatever it is you need, try to schedule this in for yourself.

> GOLD *nugget* — Rome wasn't built in a day, your business wasn't built in a day, and neither should your launch.

Remember my Starbucks story? The one where I didn't know their ordering system and got it wrong? Launching is the same way. Great launches don't happen because the business owner has some magical luck—they're following a system. And all you need to do is learn the system. Once you do, you can successfully launch (or order at Starbucks) with clarity and confidence.

YOUR RUNWAY TO LAUNCH

Launches are comprehensive, more work than you think, and necessary for your business! *The longer the runway, the better the takeoff.* But how long is long? What is the ideal launch runway? In my love-for-launching world, the most ideal runway is at least ninety days.

If you disagree with me . . . check Apple's runway! They're a well-known company that sells millions of units on launch day, but they prelaunch for *months*! Ninety days may feel like too long a time, but stop for a second and think about how fast the last thirty days have gone by in your own life. Time flies faster than you think—the more time you allow yourself to plan and prepare, the better your launch will be.

Rushing to get your offer out is going to be a shock to your system and your audience; it isn't going to help people feel comfortable or want to buy your offer. You need time to show your audience how your offer will change their life for the better.

> **GOLD** *nugget* — Launches are comprehensive, more work than you think, and necessary for your business!

THE PURPOSE OF PRELAUNCHING

The prelaunch period is crucial to how successful your launch will be. Don't rush to launch without prioritizing your prelaunch or your prelaunch event. Your prelaunch event is where your audience will join you as you launch your offer live.

Your prelaunch is all about:

- Growing your audience and reach;
- Sharing your story;
- Validating the market and your offers;
- Gathering feedback from your ideal clients;
- Learning about your audience;
- Inviting your audience to join your prelaunch event; and
- Providing your audience with an opportunity to transform their lives and solve their problems.

THE PRELAUNCH EVENT

The prelaunch event is where the magic of launching lies. Regardless of the type of prelaunch event you are hosting (a one-hour master class, a three-hour live event, a five-day challenge, or a three-part video series), the journey is the same!

Every launch begins with inviting your audience to an opportunity that is going to positively impact their lives and provide massive value. You want your audience to feel excited about the journey and the possibilities ahead of them. Remember in the Know It chapter when I talked about the importance of your why and sharing your story? A similar approach is needed for launching. People connect with story. They want to connect with the impact of your offer—the end result.

> GOLD *nugget*
>
> Your audience isn't necessarily interested in what you're selling; they're interested in *the promise of transformation* provided by what you are selling.

Questions like *What's in it for your audience? Why should they listen to you?* and *What's the end result?* become key when looking at how to structure your prelaunch event. People need to visualize what's possible for their future, they need to experience and receive real value—this is your opportunity to create that for your audience.

KEY THINGS TO KEEP IN MIND FOR YOUR PRELAUNCH EVENT

1. **Keep it relevant.** Your prelaunch event, if you've done your market research right, should be what your audience wants and *needs.*

2. **Keep it related to your final offer.** You wouldn't sign up for an hour-long webinar on how to write sales page copy if the business owner was going to sell you a course on creating a meal plan for the week ahead. I know it seems obvious, but you'd be surprised how often this disconnection happens. Take the time to make sure your prelaunch event is part of and aligned to your offer, otherwise you run the risk of confusing and losing your audience.

3. **Give yourself more time than you think you need.** Everything takes longer than you think. Plan ahead and give yourself more time than you think you'll need to organize and execute . . . especially if you are making prerecorded prelaunch content like an email video series.

4. **Lead with integrity.** Many entrepreneurs are afraid to launch because they don't want to feel sales-y. They don't want to "push" their audience or be in-your-face about sales. The answer here is simple: Don't. Don't be pushy or sales-y. Don't act in a way that compromises your integrity. But do have confidence in yourself and

your offer. Create an amazing offer and stand behind it. If you had the cure to cancer, you wouldn't sit at home, afraid to share it; you'd be shouting about it from the rooftops, trying to get everyone and anyone to listen because you knew that what you had was going to impact and transform lives. And in the spirit of integrity and launching, don't have a wait list if there is nothing to wait for. Don't say there's limited supply if there isn't. And don't create a countdown timer or deadline if there isn't one. Lead with integrity. Build trust in your relationships and launch with love.

> **GOLD** *nugget* — Everything will take you longer than you think. The longer the runway, the better the takeoff!

FIVE REASONS YOUR BUSINESS NEEDS WEBINARS

While there are many types of prelaunch events you could host to promote your launch, the highest-converting form of marketing to date are webinars. Webinars are video content delivered to your audience. You can host them live or prerecord them, but live content will always perform better. Live webinars can be your prelaunch event (they're my personal favorite) or included as a live component of your open cart. They can even be used outside of launching to build your audience and increase your email list!

I have five reasons why every business should be incorporating live webinars into their marketing and launch strategy:

1. **Webinars are the highest-converting forms of marketing.** Webinars are value-driven (or should be) because your audience gets access to you and the ability to ask questions in real time. They create a space where live engagement and feedback is celebrated and encouraged, while at the same time help to build your list with high-quality leads.

2. **Webinars create quick wins for your audience.** You want your audience to walk away from your live webinar feeling like what they've received in that one hour has given them some steps they can apply right away to start creating real transformation in their lives.

3. **Webinars position you as the expert and help build relationships with your audience.** Your attendees have to register for your live event. In doing so, they submit their email addresses (high-value information), block off the date and time in their calendars, and then carve out the time to show up and join you for one or two hours. All these steps they have to take to join you for an event position you as an expert before you even start teaching the content.

4. **Webinars teach and sell at the same time.** Effective webinars should showcase problems, crush buyer

objections, and deliver value without overwhelming your audience. The goal is to give your audience quick wins—a mindset shift, a quick takeaway they can apply right away. This helps to build know-like-trust in your ideal client because you deliver massive value that brings immediate results. The opportunity for 1:1 live conversation with a prospective customer is one of the most effective ways to engage with your audience and convert a subscriber to a buyer.

5. **Webinars broaden your impact.** Hosting a live webinar remotely allows you to connect with people around the globe, giving you a larger reach and higher engagement than you could have achieved with a local, in-person event. Your webinar can also be used as a leverage tool because you can approach different audiences or partner with other business owners, thereby benefiting from having two audiences.

> GOLD *nugget* — Webinars are the highest-converting forms of marketing.

OPEN CART

Open cart is the phase in which your online cart is open and your offer is available for purchase. This period usually lasts between three to ten days, depending on your offer and audience, with the sweet spot being between five to seven days.

To help you get a sense of what to do during a seven-day open cart period, I've included a sample schedule below:

Day 1. Open for business! If you're not shouting this from the rooftops, now is your chance! This day is all about sharing the opportunity to purchase your offer with your audience across all platforms (email and social media). You'll love building the excitement by including special bonuses for those fast-action takers who buy your offer on opening day. You've worked so hard to get here, so celebrate it loudly!

Day 2. Share the love! At this point in the launch, you're likely getting some responses to it; maybe some questions, too. This is the time to share it with the world! Share the love and drum up excitement for the launch journey you've created.

Day 3. Introduce scarcity if and only if it is real. Scarcity is a strategy used by marketers to engage an audience's subconscious survival instincts and encourage them to buy out of a misperception of limited resources. For example, someone might say something like *Buy NOW! Only ten tickets left and the offer closes in one hour!* But if after one hour you can still buy tickets, this claim is dishonest and sleazy.

Many business owners use scarcity marketing, but not all businesses provide offers that are truly limited in number. When scarcity is real, it's important to communicate that to your audience. For example, if you are hosting a live event with only twenty seats available, then you can and should tell your audience when ten spots have been sold so they can make an informed decision.

Day 3 is also a great time to invite your audience to join you for a live Q and A the next day.

Day 4. Host a live Q and A to answer questions and bust objections! Addressing the most common questions is so important. If one person has a question, you know others do, too. Make sure you answer all the questions coming in, whether it's from emails or DMs, and that you address any objections your audience has about your offer. This isn't about convincing your audience; this is about sharing the opportunity, clearing up common questions they have, and showing the possibilities so they can go from where they are now to where they want to be! The most common objections to buying are:

- money (They consider it too expensive.)
- time (It's not the right time.)

- lack of trust (They don't know, like, or trust you, yet.)

- inability to see transformation (They don't believe it will work for them.)

- lack of importance (They don't want or need it right now.)

Day 5. Go live again. Give your audience another chance to connect and get answers to their questions. Help the fence-sitters tip to your side. So many business owners want to pull back at this point in the launch. They are feeling exhausted from the process and like they're being too pushy or loud in front of their audience. But if you believe your offer can transform your audience's lives and you have done the work to provide real value, then it won't feel pushy.

You want your audience to jump in and benefit from the opportunity you are providing. You want your audience to experience the kind of transformation you know is possible, otherwise why have you done all this work to get here?

Day 6. Send a twenty-four-hour reminder. This is a loving reminder to your audience that your offer is closing at a specific date and time.

Day 7. Close your cart . . . but before you do, for the love of launching, keep your engagement high today! Go live on your social platforms and send two or three emails. Your job today is to remind your audience of the valuable opportunity that won't be available for much longer.

Special note: I strongly believe in integrity here. If you say the doors close at midnight on a certain day, then close the doors at midnight. If you've been clear about deadlines for offers and bonuses and then let clients and customers join afterward, you lose integrity and trust not only with the people who joined late but also with your audience as a whole. Unless there are proven and extremely extenuating circumstances for a customer to miss the close cart deadline, I hold firm on this. Which means yes, I have missed out on students who wanted to join MBA the day after we closed cart and who then had to wait six months before applying again. But I stand behind this rule and feel strongly about acting with integrity in your business and with your audience. Do what you say and say what you do.

GOLD *nugget* The sweet spot for open cart is five to seven days. Anything more can be exhausting for both you and your audience!

HIGHEST-CONVERTING LAUNCH DAYS

There is a pattern to launching and the open cart period. If you've launched before, you'll know this well. In the diagram below, you'll see which days you can expect to see the highest conversion rates during your launch. The highest conversions will happen the day you open cart, the day you host a live Q and A session, and the day you close cart.

HIGHEST CONVERSION DAYS

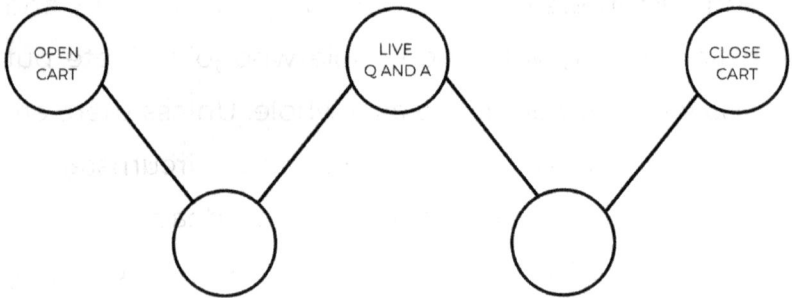

This is important to know before you go into a launch because many entrepreneurs can get discouraged after Day 1. They are on a high from their first day of sales, but then when Day 2 hits and they are not seeing as many conversions, they start thinking it is an indication of how the rest of the launch will go.

GOLD *nugget* — Know that there is a flow to launching—expecting waves will help you ride them!

POSTLAUNCH

Just because you have closed the cart doesn't mean the launch is over! This is the time to continue building the relationship with your audience, who have just gone through this launch journey with you.

In the postlaunch period, you want to show gratitude for the journey and thank your audience (both your buyers and those who didn't buy) for joining you. In this way, the postlaunch period is a great time to extend your momentum and connect with your audience.

> **GOLD** *nugget* — Show gratitude and thank your audience (both your buyers and those who didn't buy from you) for joining you on the launch journey.

ONBOARDING

Onboarding isn't just what happens after a customer hits the *Buy Now* button; it's the entire journey spent with you and your business. Knowing your clients' and customers' needs and wants will allow you to better serve them so you can make their journey with you one to remember.

Do you currently have an onboarding process for your customers or clients? Think about the question and then ask yourself how you currently *wow customers*. The journey is always more important than the destination. After all . . .

People will forget what you said. People will forget what you did. But people will never forget how you made them feel.

Maya Angelou

Your audience has just made a life-changing decision by purchasing your offer. While that may seem dramatic, it's what you promised. Whatever opportunity you are providing, whether you're selling $5 products or $30,000 coaching containers, you have promised to transform your customers' lives, so their investment should be respected and honored.

In a launch, this is the time to over-deliver: send out immediate bonuses and any other exciting details to those who purchased. You want to wow your new customers and clients and make them feel good about their investment.

> GOLD *nugget*
>
> Your onboarding (and offboarding) process is one of the most important steps in your customer's journey! Ignoring or devaluing the significance of this is a mistake that will cost you long term.

DEBRIEFING: THE MOST IMPORTANT STEP OF A LAUNCH

Working behind the scenes on many launches, I know one thing for sure . . . no two are the same! Regardless of how many times you have launched, the size of your team, or the product or service you are launching, each one will always be different. Every launch will give you more insight into your customers, your product, and your business.

There is so much work that goes into a live launch, so don't waste the process by skipping the most important step: the launch debrief.

A launch debrief gives you the opportunity to examine the impact of your launch by looking at what worked, what didn't, and what you would do differently next time. Your first step is to survey your audience. You want to learn from both your buyers and those who didn't buy from you. Use their answers to these questions to adjust your offers and launch strategy, so you can transform and better serve moving forward.

Completing a launch debrief gives you the opportunity to deepen your connection with your audience. By finding out what their limiting beliefs and objections are, you can give yourself the time and space needed to bust through them and deliver a better approach next time.

GOLD *nugget*

No two launches are ever the same. Every launch will give you insights into your customers, your offers, you, and your business.

KEY PERFORMANCE INDICATORS

It's so important to know your numbers in business. Key performance indicators (KPIs) are quantifiable and actionable measurements of the success of your business. They are critical numbers tied directly to the goals for your launch. They are not meant to provide vague nice-to-knows or overly exhaustive reports.

The main thing you want to learn is whether your launch resonated with your audience. Look at the numbers before your launch and the numbers after. Did you gain email subscribers? Did you see an increase in followers and engagement with your audience on your social accounts?

Look at the impact goals for your launch. Did you achieve them? What was the total revenue gained? Did you generate recurring revenue, either through membership, retention, or product sales? What were your launch costs? How much did you spend on ads, giveaways, bonuses, and affiliate payouts?

What was your email list conversion rate? What were your bounce and cart abandonment rates?

Knowing these numbers will help you see the overall picture of your launch's performance and implement strategies to improve your next one.

> **GOLD** *nugget* — Numbers don't lie. As a business owner, it's so important to identify and understand the KPIs that contribute to the growth of your business.

IT'S NOT ONE AND DONE

For twenty years, I've worked behind the scenes for many businesses.

I had helped clients with four- to six-figure launches for years, but my first launch for my own signature program brought in a whopping $500. I would like to classify it as a success, but considering the fact that my husband was my only buyer, I don't think it counts.

Looking back, I can see my expectations were *way* too high at the time! I knew how to execute a high-converting launch. In my mind, my own launch was going to be easy. I was a one-woman show with a big vision then.

I set up my prelaunch master class and had twenty people join, which was great considering my email list size was thirteen subscribers and most of those were family. I went live for a full hour, nervous as heck the whole time, and only afterward did I see messages from attendees trying to tell me there was no sound! Needless to say, the entire live event was a flop, minus the one conversion, and I was left feeling so discouraged.

I have two points to this story. The first is that a launch that fails to convert isn't a flop. It is an opportunity to listen, learn, and adapt. The second point is to not give up. While I could have easily thrown in the towel, embarrassed by the perceived failure, and never hosted a public event again, I had a bigger burning *why* inside. I knew my knowledge and experience could positively impact the people I work with. I just had to build the confidence to do it again!

I learned, made changes, better prepared, and four months later, I relaunched and brought in $5,000. Three months after that, I relaunched again and brought in $25,000. The next launch brought in over $50,000. If I had let that first launch get the better of me and closed up shop, I wouldn't have hit six figures just one and a half years after starting my business in that corner office with the concrete floors.

I tell you this story to give you hope. If I had given up, I wouldn't have helped the entrepreneurs I've had the honor of working with. Maybe the entrepreneurs I've worked with might have considered launching a hill too big to climb alone and would have given up, too. Or worse, they would have never seen the possibilities that were in front of them or believed in themselves enough to birth their dreams into the world.

Maybe you're one of those entrepreneurs reading this. If you've had an unsuccessful launch or you have moments of doubt, wondering what you're doing, go back to your why, to your purpose, to your heart. Open yourself up to the possibilities in front of you; not behind or beside you, but what is in front of you and lean in.

GOLD *nugget*

It's not one and done. When you have focus, determination, and a whole lot of heart, big things are possible. You've got this!

A LAUNCH THAT FAILS TO CONVERT IS NOT A FAILURE

Remember, even a launch that fails to convert at all is not a failure. It's a learning opportunity to gather information and find out how you can better serve your audience moving forward.

I learned this well in the art world, too! As artists, we would pay hundreds, sometimes thousands of dollars to be in certain art shows. Some shows we would sell out, bringing in large profits, while at others we would break even, earning just enough to cover the costs of the show, travel, hotel, rentals, and other expenses. Then there were some shows where we wouldn't sell a thing and would be in the hole for expenses. But every show, regardless of its success, was an opportunity to learn more about our audience. It was an opportunity to see who we were connecting with, who was interested in our work, which markets were "buying markets," and which markets were there for weekend strolls and park visits.

Every show was an opportunity to learn more about our audience, our customers, our work, and how what we did connected with our audience.

Just because a customer doesn't buy from you at the time of your launch (or show, in the art world example), it doesn't mean they won't ever. A no may actually be a not-right-now. My real-world example of this is our experience as exhibitors at an art show in Toronto. The show charged a $5,000 exhibitor fee and we made only $1,000 in sales at the live event. Three weeks later, however, we sold $10,000 worth of privately commissioned art to collectors who had seen our work at the Toronto show and chatted with us at our booth.

A launch is no different. It is an opportunity to learn more about the people you are doing this for and for them to learn more about you. By launching, you expose more people to your business, connect with your ideal clients, and discover how you can better serve current and future customers.

> GOLD *nugget* A launch that fails to convert is not a failure, it's a learning opportunity. Use it wisely!

CELEBRATE FAILURE

Sara Blakely, CEO of SPANX, grew up in a home that celebrated failure. In a video, she shared that each week, her dad would ask her and her brother at the dinner table if they had failed at something. The best part was that if she admitted she had, he high-fived her.

Failure is something to be celebrated, which is why every week inside MBA, we celebrate Failure Fridays! We welcome failure because it means you've gone out on a skinny limb and tried. It means you are putting yourself out there, doing what you are meant to do in this world, and finding your way on your business journey.

So many entrepreneurs don't start businesses or launch the dream that lives inside of them because they fear failure. But if you can redefine failure and find gold nuggets along the way, life will open up to you in ways you wouldn't know were possible if you had never tried.

IT'S NOT EASY, BUT IT'S WORTH IT

I know how hard it is to put your all into something and then not have it succeed. To truly believe you are doing your best for yourself and your family, and not have it work out. When the pressure is on you to make it all better, to succeed at doing what you love, what you truly believe will make a difference in this world . . . the stakes are *high*.

Sometimes things don't work out the way you planned; sometimes you hit a roadblock or life presents you with a challenge that knocks you down. But you have the choice to pick yourself back up, examine and assess your surroundings, and pivot and tweak to make your approach better next time.

As renowned entrepreneur Neil Patel says, "[e]very company, no matter how small, has the opportunity to revolutionize their business. Do something none of your competitors have ever done before, take a position that's bold and imaginative, paint a picture of the future that your customers *want* to live in, and then put your whole company into motion creating that vision."

If you have a vision, the courage to lead, and focus on serving your people, you will make your vision a reality. It's not easy, but it's worth it!

GOLD nuggets
LAUNCH TIPS

- Launching is a journey, not a destination. Enjoy the ride!

- The longer the runway, the better the takeoff—everything will take you longer than you think!

- Expect the unexpected.

- Lead with integrity—do what you say and say what you do.

- A launch that fails to convert is not a failure.

- Launch it messy.

Homefun
EMBRACING IMPERFECTION

If we wait until we're ready, we'll be waiting for the rest of our lives.

Lemony Snicket

As business owners and entrepreneurs, we can bottleneck ourselves and our efforts by getting distracted by new and exciting ideas (sometimes referred to as shiny object syndrome). We get in our own way by not feeling "ready." There is always going to be another shiny object to focus on: a new offer, another tweak to your current offer idea, or a way to make what you do better. But done is better than perfect and it's important to get your work out into the world. Your ideal clients are waiting for you, searching for the solution you offer. Launch it messy, launch it imperfectly, and do what you are meant to do in this world.

Ask yourself, what is holding you back from launching your offer into the world? Is it the price of the offer? Are you feeling stuck or unclear about who your ideal client is? Are you waiting until your email list is bigger? Or is your offer done and ready, but you haven't released it yet because it doesn't *feel* like the right time? If you've answered yes to any of these questions, go back. Go to the sections in this book that will help you work through these roadblocks. Pick a price for your offer, do some market research to gain clarity on your ideal client, and don't wait for your list to get bigger to launch (launching is how you build your list, after all!). There will never be a right time for anything, so do it now. Launch it messy. Done is better than perfect!

And if you find yourself, like many creative entrepreneurs, distracted by shiny objects? Use the space I've provided here to dump them all out of your brain and choose *one* of them to focus on. Pick the one thing that lights you up, sparks joy in your heart, and will transform your ideal clients' lives. Launch the one thing knowing that this list of shiny objects is here for you to come back to.

Shiny Objects:

LOVE IT

Gratitude changes everything.

Earl Gerson

This world needs your creative mind, your kind heart, and *you*, living in your limitless potential, shining your light for others to see.

Many of the clients and students I help are women entrepreneurs. As such, part of that is helping women in business who menstruate. If you're reading this book and don't think this is for you because you don't menstruate, stay with me. This information is for everyone and should be learned and talked about more.

In this chapter, we dive into your infradian rhythm and how it affects your life, your business, and your launches; how to launch in flow; and the importance of cultivating gratitude.

LOVE YOUR FLOW

Learning how to leverage your infradian rhythm for success and well-being, by connecting with your inner timing and using your body as your guide, has massive benefits!

> GOLD *nugget* | When you live out of sync with your infradian rhythm, you damage both your physical and mental health.

While I'm not an expert on the topic, I can share some wisdom I've gained through my research and personal experiences into each of the phases of the infradian rhythm and the impact it can have on your life when you start applying that knowledge to your business. After reading Alisa Vitti's book *In the Flo*, and incorporating this cyclical way of living into my business structure, it's been a game changer, and I hope it will be for you, too!

WHAT IS THE INFRADIAN RHYTHM?

Most of us are familiar with the circadian rhythm, which is a twenty-four hour cycle that controls biological functions. The amazing gift of female biology, though, is that we have two clocks—the circadian rhythm and the infradian rhythm! The infradian rhythm is a twenty-eight-day cycle that regulates the menstrual cycle.

Research has shown the infradian rhythm significantly affects the chemistry of your brain on a monthly basis, which in turn impacts how interested you are in certain tasks.

Knowing this information is so amazing because it can influence the way we can plan our schedule and our launches to better support our minds and bodies!

There are four phases to your infradian rhythm and each has its own characteristics which can guide you when planning your business and launch.

1. **Follicular Phase:** This phase occurs seven to ten days after your period. The theme of this phase is preparation. Your strength in this phase is creativity. In your business and launch, this is when you enter your think tank; where you dream big, strategize, and plan specific goals for the weeks leading up to your launch.

2. **Ovulatory Phase:** This phase lasts three or four days and is all about opening up. Your strengths in this phase are communication and collaboration. It's time to socialize and increase your engagement with your audience. Pitch collaborations and guest speaking engagements, host webinars, and generally get out into the world. This is the perfect time to launch!

3. **Luteal Phase:** During the ten to fourteen days between ovulation and your period, your strengths are completion and detailed work. This is the phase where it's best to get organized. You will want to wrap up your launch and onboarding process, and complete the admin tasks and goals you planned in the follicular phase. This is also a great time to look at your KPIs.

4. **Menstrual Phase:** Bring on the chocolate! I mean, rest . . . This phase lasts three to seven days and is a time to relax, debrief, and reflect. Release what no longer serves you, set new intentions, and trust your intuition to guide you this week! This is the time to survey your audience, debrief your launch, and make notes about what worked, what didn't, and how you will pivot for the next launch. During this phase, it's important to trust your instincts . . . Listen to your gut and your heart.

We are meant to live in rhythm with this natural cycle. Living out of sync with your natural rhythms is taxing for your system; you're more likely to suffer from stress and burnout when you're in constant grind mode!

The last thing you want to do is launch during your menstrual phase. As the owner and visionary of your business, you get to plan how and when you launch. But working against the timing of your body's natural rhythms will feel more challenging, overwhelming, and stressful.

PLANNING YOUR LAUNCH WITH YOUR INFRADIAN RHYTHM

Infradian Phase	Launch Theme	Launch Actions
Follicular	Lay the Foundation	The best time to plan your promotions and launches. Get the big vision organized.
Ovulatory	Reach Out & Connect	The best time to reach your audience, connect, collaborate, and *launch*!
Luteal	Wrap Up	The best time to wrap up your plans and projects. Close your cart and onboard new clients, students, or members.
Menstrual	Debrief	The best time to debrief, reflect, rest, and set new intentions.

WHERE TO START?

Get curious about your body and your business. Look at ways to optimize your life by following *your* natural rhythms. There is no one-size-fits-all—in life or business! Own your unique power and help others own theirs. When you allow yourself to be thoughtful in this way with your business planning, you give others permission to do the same. Support your body by building a business that fits *you*. Health is wealth!

The best way to start is to track your energy levels. Look at your year ahead and break it down into quarterly planning. Then look at the months in each quarter and plan out your weeks based on your infradian rhythm. Schedule your launches, major promotions, and in-person events when it makes the best sense for you physically.

The key is to be kind to yourself; embrace the impact this can have on your productivity and your health, go with your flow, and keep it simple.

By being mindful of your phases and your corresponding energy levels, you can optimize your output, feel better connected to your work, reduce your stress, and increase your capacity to welcome more of what you want in life.

THE COOL FACTOR OF THE FLOW

Our bodies are pretty amazing to begin with, but tapping into your natural rhythm gets you access to information that will help you live in flow!

My infradian cycle is like clockwork. It has synced with the lunar cycle, so that the start and end of my infradian cycle occurs during certain lunar phases.

But twice a year, when I launch MBA, my menstrual phase comes one week early. Here's why this is cool . . . it also happens to be one or two weeks earlier than most of the women who join MBA. Meaning: when the women in my coaching container are menstruating and need more support and care, I'm able to provide it!

Because while they are in their menstrual phase, I have moved into my follicular phase.

What's even cooler is, this isn't unusual. In history, women who menstruated a week earlier than other women in their community were priestesses and healers . . . committed to doing deep, meaningful work in the world that serves others. These women have acted as bridges, offering loving guidance and support to other women so they can reach their highest potential.

How cool is that?

Knowing what your body does and how that impacts your life and business is powerful information.

That's why in Week 8 of MBA, we talk about "launching in the flow." We learn about the infradian rhythm and how to build a business around your life and body, not the other way around. Because when you can plan your days, weeks, and launch in the flow of your infradian cycle, you support your physical and mental health . . . and that's pretty cool.

GOLD nuggets

1. We are meant to be in rhythm with our infradian cycles.

2. Try not to launch during your menstrual phase if you can help it, because you will be working against your natural rhythm. While you can do it, it will be better for your mind and body if you don't.

3. If you are working against your natural rhythms, find ways to build in more self-care and compassion so you don't suffer from overwhelm, stress, and exhaustion. Take a walk, have a bath, or cozy up with a tea at the end of your day.

GRATITUDE

Much of our time and energy is spent pursuing things we currently don't have. Gratitude reverses those priorities and helps us appreciate the people and things we already have. According to research collected by Harvard Medical School, "gratitude helps people feel more positive emotions, relish good experiences, improve their health, deal with adversity, and build strong relationships."

Gratitude is a powerful force and can have real and lasting positive effects on your physical and emotional well-being. Here is a list of ways that gratitude can positively impact your life:

- increases happiness and positive emotions
- creates more satisfaction for what you have instead of always reaching for something new or focusing on what you lack
- improves health, sleep, and resiliency

- lowers inflammation
- lessens the likeliness of burnout
- encourages the development of patience, humility, and wisdom

With these positive effects at stake, it's easy to see the value in finding ways to incorporate gratitude into your daily routine. There are many ways to cultivate gratitude in your life, so I've included some simple strategies to get you started here:

- Say it out loud. Every morning when I wake up, before my feet touch the ground, I say out loud three things I am grateful for.
- Write it down and share it. Love notes or gratitude notes are a wonderful way to cultivate and share gratitude. As I was writing this chapter, my daughter gave me a note that read, *You've got this, Mama. I love you.* This simple note filled my heart with gratitude for receiving it and my daughter's for sharing it.
- Keep a gratitude journal. Writing can be therapeutic, as it invites you to pause and reflect on what you are grateful for. Be consistent; pick a time each week to sit down and reflect.
- Meditate on what you're grateful for. Make it part of your morning or bedtime routine so that each day you have space for it.

- Be mindful of your five senses. How does each one enhance your life?
- Put up visual reminders to practice gratitude. Sticky love notes around your home or office are a fun way to cultivate gratitude in your home.
- Be on the lookout for opportunities to feel grateful— where attention goes, energy flows. Focus on the positive and your life will be filled with moments you can be grateful for.

Gratitude opens the door to abundance! Every time another cohort goes through MBA, my heart bursts with love and gratitude, witnessing these amazing women as they transform over the course of the program.

Like Carley, who decided to launch a signature program that featured her products. She sold out all the available spots before launch, built a wait list for the next one, and created a community of women who *love* her products!

Or Stacey, a personal trainer who had to pivot online because of COVID-19 and created The Everyday Athlete membership program, which allowed her to feel inspired by her work again and able to connect with her clients regardless of lockdown measures.

Or Emily, a copywriter who struggled with launching before joining the program, but once inside, sold out her beta round and has had one of the most successful launches to date, reaching consistent revenues of $10,000 a month.

Or Laura, a coach who launched a signature program, a podcast, and a quiz to build her list, connect with her ideal clients, and build a community of women who want to find their unique voice and rise while rooted in their authentic selves.

Or Jessica, a teacher whose love of entrepreneurship got her thinking outside of the school system. She launched a youth entrepreneurship program so successful that she had investors backing the program in order to get it into the hands of as many young people as possible.

Or Lori, an Iyengar yoga instructor who also pivoted online because of COVID-19 by collaborating with a partner in another country to create a year-long yoga program featuring guest instructors from India and accessed by students from around the world!

Or Sarah, an herbalist with a product-based business, who niched down and created a signature program and workshops to diversify her income, help her ideal clients, and highlight her products. Through the program, Sarah discovered she could change her business structure to work in flow with the seasons. At the time of writing this book, she is on track to "winter" with her business in accordance with this season.

Or Vanessa, a lawyer who saw a need in the market and created a program for entrepreneurs to learn all the legal aspects of running their business.

Or Traci, a university professor who runs a nonprofit that creates wellness bundles to help conscious-minded teachers better support their students to effectively provide education that transforms.

These stories inspire me every day. They are the why behind what I do. These women and their stories fill my heart with gratitude: gratitude for the spark that started this business, for my determination to not give up after my first launch "failure," and for both the entrepreneurs I have had the honor of helping and the ones that are on their way.

FIND YOUR ANCHOR

Who are your biggest supporters? Who cheers you on, regardless of the outcome? Who has your back? Who stands with you through thick and thin? Who believes in you when you may not even believe in yourself?

When I was one week away from my manuscript deadline, my three kids and Kiel cheered me on. They literally stood in the living room and cheered me down the hall to my office: "You can do it; you can do it." As I write these words, the tears well up in my eyes, and I am filled with gratitude for my family's love and support. They always believe in me, have my back, and cheer me on when I need it most. They are my biggest supporters, my anchors in times of storm, my "why" and motivation for what I do and how I do it.

Maybe for you it's a childhood friend, a bestie, a coach, your blood family, your soul family, your partner, or your chosen family. Whoever that is for you, find your anchor. Anchor into that goodness. Anchor into those who lift you up, believe in you, and cheer you on. Doing so will fill your heart with love, your mind with motivation, and your soul with gratitude.

Homefun

RHYTHM AND GRATITUDE

We covered some points in this chapter that are easily forgotten or overlooked. But when we focus on and honor them, they can make a big difference to our health and well-being. Take this opportunity for yourself:

- Block out your infradian cycle in your calendar for the next three months. Try to plan your business, meetings, and launching around your cycle and note any changes you notice.
- Implement a gratitude practice. Start today by sharing a note expressing gratitude with someone in your world. If you can't think of something to write, feel free to share this note to the first person that pops into your mind when you read it: *Thank you for who you are being in this world.*
- Share the love. Gratitude changes everything!

BITS & BOBS

The process of writing this book was a challenge for me. One of my core values is quality and I wanted to make sure quality is what I delivered. My biggest challenge in getting this guide out was knowing that by the time it's printed, I may have found newer and better ways to communicate how to help you along your business journey. In order to push through that hesitation, I did what I always recommend: I got myself a mentor and a coach, both of whom had been down this road before and could guide my way.

I joined YGTMedia's Author Generator Society to help me birth this book. I knew I had the vision, but needed the resources, support, and accountability baked into their step-by-step program to get this guide out into the world.

Along the way, I also invested with Dive Heart First Coaching, so I could align my mindset and business for abundance, joy, and massive success.

Investing in yourself is not just a gift for yourself, it's a gift for those around you.

In this last chapter, I've included some bits and bobs I believe are necessary and important to the launching process, but didn't fit well enough in any of the previous chapters. So here's a little bonus information for you!

NO IS A COMPLETE SENTENCE

Stephen Covey, author of *The 7 Habits of Highly Effective People*, once said: "[y]ou have to decide what your highest priorities are and have the courage—pleasantly, smilingly, and nonapologetically—to say 'no' to other things. And the way you do that is by having a bigger 'yes' burning inside."

What you say no to is as important as what you say yes to. As a "yes" person, a natural-born people-pleaser, a type-A determined individual, the word *no* is underused in my vocabulary. For the longest time, I thought saying no meant that I couldn't do something, and I have always been out to prove that I could. But as I learn more about myself and others around me, I realize that no doesn't mean you can't do it; it can also mean you *won't* do it, and that holds a very different meaning.

> **GOLD** ~~nugget~~ What you say no to is as important as what you say yes to.

I've said yes to many things, and it's resulted in a business I'm proud of, clients I love to work with, and work that fuels me. But I've also said no to things I would have previously said yes to. Saying no has meant not doing the things that don't fuel me, not working with people who don't align with my values, and standing up for my worth. Because when you believe in your worth and show up for yourself, others do too.

Even if you're just starting out with your business and feel like the only option is to say yes, know that saying yes now doesn't mean saying yes forever. You always have the option of choosing differently, and you can always, and should always, consider what saying no means, too.

TAKE BACK YOUR WEEKEND

You built this business to be more present, have more freedom, and create wealth while doing what you love. Yet every Sunday I see *so many* social media posts encouraging you to spend the day prepping for the week ahead.

I would like to take this opportunity to invite you *not* to.

Take back your weekend, your time with your family, yourself, your life, and the things you love *outside* of your business! Leave the business at your desk and put your work brain on silent mode.

Instead, I invite you to use Fridays to complete what I like to call "A Week in Review." Look at what you set out to accomplish that week: Did you check off your big needle-movers? What got done? Then identify what didn't get done and where time was wasted. Use this information to prepare and plan your next week *before* you leave your office and embark on your weekend.

> GOLD *nugget* — Plan your next week on Friday *before* you head out for the weekend so you can put your work brain on silent mode.

Every time I wrap up my week, I feel organized and focused for the next week. It's not weighing on my brain over the weekend, because I know I've put in the work to prepare. Take back your weekend and enjoy the time away from your work brain. You will come back to your work feeling refreshed, recharged, and ready to take on your week.

RED FLAGS AND TRUSTING YOUR BOUNDARIES

This is sage advice for anyone! Red flags are moments that make you pause. Something might raise the hairs on the back of your neck or give you a "gut feeling" that something is off. Whether it's with your clients, your students, your customers, or your team, don't be in the habit of collecting red flags. Address problems directly, hold your boundaries, and most importantly, trust your intuition.

GOLD *nugget* — Trust your intuition and don't be in the habit of collecting red flags!

I have encountered several red flags in my time. There have been times when it almost made me give up entirely. I have felt like a small fish in a big, shark-filled ocean. If you've been bitten before and you're reading this, I'm sorry. It's sad, disappointing, frustrating, and not okay. But it is always darkest before dawn and every experience is an opportunity to learn and grow.

Past red flags have taught me to trust my boundaries. After one unfortunate experience, I had just finished reading Michalowicz's *The Pumpkin Plan* and decided to aggressively curate my client list. The decision was terrifying, because I was the sole income-earner at the time and I was reducing 75 percent of our recurring income. Two months later, I relaunched my program, choosing to work only with heart-centered entrepreneurs, and watched my business hit its first six-figure year.

STONE SOUP

In business and life, there is wisdom in knowing that going with others gets you where you need to go. My family loves reading the beautiful children's book, *Stone Soup* by Jon J. Muth, because it teaches the importance of collaboration. When the villagers in the story decide to trust the newcomers and contribute ingredients to the soup pot, their collective generosity creates a delicious meal that serves them all.

Business collaboration is the same. Not everyone will be a collaborator, but keep your heart open, give what you've got, do one thing to make this world a better place, and you'll see the butterfly effect happen.

FINAL GOLD
nuggets

- Stand up for yourself, your business, and your boundaries.

- Lead with Integrity. Be the leader you want to see in this world.

- No clients are better than bad clients. The clients who don't respect you and suck the life from you are the clients who will slow your growth, drain you, and distract you from your goals.

- Protect your intellectual property. Vanessa Locicero is my heart-centered Soul Attorney™, and she has my back. Find a lawyer who can have yours!

- Surrender and know that everything happens for a reason.

- Keep your energy positive: send love to the ones who have hurt you, and know they were doing the best they could with what they had.

- Once you know better, do better.

- Be open to collaboration, but know that not everyone is a collaborator.

- Don't let one bad-apple experience spoil the bunch. Pick yourself back up, dust yourself off, and get back in the game. You didn't come here to remain small; you came here to expand gracefully to your highest potential.

And with that, I want to leave you with some final words . . .

You are always one decision away from a totally different life.

The biggest and scariest decisions always level up your life.
What got you here, where you are now, won't get you to where
you want to go.
You are here for a reason.
Trust your gut, your intuition and your heart's guidance.
You are worthy of all the success and ease that comes your way.
Everyone benefits when you care for yourself.
You are totally worthy and deserving of the life you dream of.
Own your unique power and help others own theirs too.
Do it differently.
When one of us shines, we all shine.
Do not dim your light. Shine bright for everyone to see!

Amanda XO

GLOSSARY

beta offer—An offer that is new to your audience. The purpose of a beta offer is testing the effectiveness of your idea on your users. Use the feedback you've gained from your users to tweak and modify the offer for a larger product launch.

call to action (CTA)—An action you ask your audience to take when you share content with them. Examples include liking or saving your post, subscribing to a newsletter, replying to your email, sharing with others, and making a purchase.

client—Someone who has bought a product or service from you. At The Monarch & Co., we have 1:1 coaching clients, Deep Dive & Roadmap session clients, and clients of our full-service digital marketing agency.

content pillars—The themes of your content marketing that you use to create a cohesive brand identity. Examples include inspiration, education, personal, entertainment, promotion, and social proof. They are sometimes referred to as buckets.

conversion—When your audience acts based on your marketing efforts. For example, when a follower becomes a subscriber or a subscriber moves from a lead to a customer. The rate of conversion is measurable and knowing it is extremely valuable to your business strategy.

core values—A set of guiding principles that influence the way you make decisions, how you view the world, and guide both your personal and professional behavior. Your core values explain who you are at the deepest level.

core why—Your biggest motivator and the reason why what you do is important. Your core why lives beneath the surface of everything you do, keeps you up at night, and motivates you to keep moving forward.

Deep Dive & Roadmap session—A two-hour 1:1 session with me where we work through a series of questions that cover all the parts of your big vision and business. From the big picture to the nitty-gritty, we cover it all. By diving deeply into where you are now and where you want to go, I provide you with a custom road map to collapse time and gain clarity. It's a step-by-step plan with overall recommendations and specific next steps to get where you want to go. I love the scenic route while traveling, but in business, I'm all about the optimized route!

heart-centered entrepreneur—This type of entrepreneur positively influences society while running profitable businesses. They create value for their customers and communities with a desire to make a bigger, better impact on the world.

homefun—End-of-chapter exercises that push you to ask important questions that will grow your business. It's like home-work, but it's fun!

ideal client avatar—The detailed profile of the type of customer who is ideal to work with and ideal for your business' product or offer.

infradian rhythm—The twenty-eight-day cycle that regulates the menstrual cycle. There are four phases to your infradian rhythm, each with its own characteristics that you can use to plan your business and launch strategies more effectively.

key performance indicators (KPIs)—Quantifiable and action-able measurements of the success of your business. They are critical numbers tied directly to the goals of your launch.

launch debrief—The act of examining the impact of your launch by looking at what worked, what didn't, and what you would do differently next time in the postlaunch period after you have closed your cart. This is the most critical step of your launch, because if done right, it will give you valuable insights into how to achieve success in the future.

launch effect—Sometimes more negatively referred to as a launch hangover, this is the period of time after a launch where you need to practice rest and recovery.

lead magnets—A (usually) free resource that you promote to your subscribers in exchange for their email addresses. Some-times also referred to as a freebie or an opt-in, it is an integral marketing tool for your online business.

live launch—A style of launching where the content is delivered live to your audience through a challenge, webinar, or master class.

low-value activities—Activities that are necessary and important to your business' ability to function, but that should be delegated so you can spend time on activities that move your business forward. They include responding to emails and inquiries, scheduling meetings, and updating spreadsheets.

market research—Research done to gather information about niche markets and customer types. Insights from this type of research help you to better understand your audience, as well as how your products and services help your ideal clients. Market research is critical to understanding your market base and which business strategy to use.

mission statement—The why behind what you do and why you exist. It is similar to your core why, but it's a shorter statement that speaks to your purpose in the present moment. You come up with it by looking at how you help people and asking yourself why what you do is important.

Monarch Business Academy (MBA)—My epic, three-month-long business, mindset, and launch accelerator signature program. Inside a cocoon of magic, we work through the Signature 8 Method to build and launch a business and life you love.

niche market—The segment of a larger market that has specific characteristics. You adapt your strategy to these niche markets to help you better understand, communicate, and connect with them.

niche product—The product or offer you are selling to your niche market because it meets their needs or wants specifically.

onboarding—The journey your clients or customers embark on when they purchase an offer from you or convert from a follower to a subscriber. I like to think of the process as the welcome party to your community!

open cart—The period of time when your offer is available for purchase, lasting anywhere from twenty-four hours to seven days.

postlaunch—The period of time right after closing your cart during your launch. This is the time to continue building a relationship with your audience, as they've just gone through the launch journey with you.

prelaunch—The period that starts three to four weeks before you open cart and includes your prelaunch event.

prelaunch event—The event where you will officially launch your offer to your audience. It is often delivered live in the form of a webinar, master class, or challenge.

profit—The income remaining after the subtraction of expenses and costs.

red flag—Moments in your life or business dealings that make you pause because they don't feel right.

signature offer—The unique offer or service you have created that takes your clients or students on a journey of transformation to achieve the results they want and need in their life and business.

student—Entrepreneurs who have joined Monarch Business Academy.

vision board—A visual representation of your dreams and goals, made either digitally or using paper and glue.

vision statement—What you see for the future of your business. It defines your purpose and goals, combines your company values, and is often timeless.

webinar—Video content delivered to your audience. They can be prerecorded, but live ones are the highest-converting form of marketing to date and as such, relevant to every business.

ADDITIONAL RESOURCES

RESOURCES

www.themonarchandco.com/bookresources

COLLEAGUES

Dr. Paula Moore, content storyteller
https://ivorypencil.com/

Jenn Walker, Dive Heart First Coaching
@diveheartfirst
https://diveheartfirst.com/

Vanessa Locicero, JD, heart-centered Soul Attorney™
@soul.attorney
https://www.thesoulattorney.com/

BOOKS

Covey, Stephen R. *The 7 Habits of Highly Effective People*. RosettaBooks, 2004.

Iyengar, B.K.S. *Light on Life: The Yoga Journey to Wholeness, Inner Peace, and Ultimate Freedom*. Rodale, 2006.

Michalowicz, Mike. *The Pumpkin Plan: A Simple Strategy to Grow a Remarkable Business in Any Field*. Portfolio, 2012.

Muth, Jon J. *Stone Soup*. Scholastic Press, 2010.

Vitti, Alisa. *In the Flo*. HarperCollins, 2020

Sinek, Simon. *Start with Why: How Great Leaders Inspire Everyone to Take Action*. Portfolio, 2009.

Walker, Jeff. *Launch: An Internet Millionaire's Secret Formula to Sell Almost Anything Online, Build a Business You Love, and Live the Life of Your Dreams*. Morgan James Publishing, 2014.

ARTICLES

"19 Compelling Women Entrepreneurs Statistics for 2022." What To Become (blog). September 21, 2021. https://whattobecome.com/blog/women-entrepreneurs-statistics/

Fulton, Bethany. "The Benefits of Gratitude and How to Get Started." Healthline. October 27, 2020.

Healthbeat. "Giving Thanks Can Make You Happier." Harvard Health Publishing. August 14, 2021.

Jabr, Ferris. "How Does a Caterpillar Turn into a Butterfly?" *Scientific American*. August 10, 2012.

Kiniulis, Marius. "12 Entrepreneur Statistics You Need to Know." MARKINBLOG.com. March 23, 2022. https://www.markinblog.com/entrepreneur-statistics/

Loder, Vanessa. "The Power of Vision—What Entrepreneurs Can Learn From Olympic Athletes." *Forbes*. July 23, 2014.

Patel, Neil. "7 Product Launch Strategies to Create Buzz Around Your Business." Neilpatel.com (blog). Neil Patel Digital, LLC. 2022. https://neilpatel.com/blog/product-launch-strategies/

Vitti, Alisa. "Infradian Rhythm: Your Guide to a Perfect Cycle." Flo Living (blog). Last updated October 25, 2021. https://www.floliving.com/infradian-rhythm/

REPORTS

Cukier, W., Mo, G. Y., Chavoushi, Z. H., Blanchette, S., Noshiravani, R. (2021). *The State of Women's Entrepreneurship in Canada 2021*. Women Entrepreneurship Knowledge Hub. https://wekh.ca/wp-content/uploads/2021/06/State_of_Womens_Entrepreneurship_in_Canada_2021.pdf

VIDEOS

Bob Ross: Happy Accidents, Betrayal & Greed (Joshua Rofé, director, 2021, Netflix)

"Dr. Joe Dispenza | Practice The Gratitude (The Extraordinary Power Of Gratitude)" excerpt (JustMotivation, published May 20, 2020, YouTube, https://youtu.be/lYQb4SWmD_4)

"Gratitude Changes Everything w/ Errol Gerson" podcast excerpt (Chris Do, host, The Futur, published October 22, 2019, YouTube, https://youtu.be/YOq_VPgK6t0)

"How Great Leaders Inspire Action" talk (Simon Sinek, speaker, September 2009, TEDxPuget Sound)

Self Made: Inspired by the Life of Madam C.J. Walker (Kasi Lemmons, director, 2020, Netflix)

"SPANX Founder Sara Blakely on Overcoming Fear of Failure in Business" talk (Tony Robbins, interviewer, published June 23, 2020, YouTube, accessed February 2022, https://youtu.be/9JrAojUqMvQ)

"What Oprah Learned from Jim Carrey" clip, originally aired October 12, 2011 (*The Oprah Winfrey Show*, 1986–2011, Oprah.com)

INSPIRING QUOTES

Bhagavad Gita

Georgia O'Keeffe

Henry Ford

Lemony Snicket

Lisa Hammond

Maya Angelou

Nathaniel Hawthorne

Paul Gardner

Rebecca Campbell

Seth Godin

LAUNCH TESTIMONIALS PAGE

https://www.monarchbusinessacademy.com/monarch-love

YGTMedia Co. is a blended boutique publishing house for mission-driven humans. We help seasoned and emerging authors "birth their brain babies" through a supportive and collaborative approach. Specializing in narrative nonfiction and adult and children's empowerment books, we believe that words can change the world, and we intend to do so one book at a time.

🌐 ygtmedia.co/publishing

📷 @ygtmedia.company

f @ygtmedia.co

www.ingramcontent.com/pod-product-compliance
Lightning Source LLC
Chambersburg PA
CBHW071604210326
41597CB00019B/3402